PRAYERS FOR FAMILIES

Contents

Preface   *page* 9

1 Prologue   13
  (i) Introduction   13
  (ii) A Minister's prayer   13

2 Family Prayers for use on weekdays   16
  (i) Introduction   16
  (ii) Seven Morning prayers   17
  (iii) Seven Evening prayers   29
  (iv) The Lord's Prayer extended   48

3 Prayers for use on the Lord's Day   53
  (i) Introduction   53
  (ii) Two Morning prayers   54
  (iii) A Midday prayer   58
  (iv) Two Evening prayers   60
  (v) Two prayers for before and after hearing
     the Word   65
  (vi) Four prayers for before and after the
     Lord's Supper   67
  (vii) Three prayers for the Church   76

4 Prayers for use on Church Festivals   81
  (i) Introduction   81
  (ii) Six prayers from Christmas to Saints' Days   81

5 Personal Petitions for growth in spirituality   90
  (i) Introduction   90

(ii) Personal Prayers for the grace of God 91
    1. For illumination and knowledge 91
    2. For faith and trust in God 93
    3. For power to live by faith in Christ 94
    4. For repentance 97
    5. For humility 99
    6. For tenderness of heart 100
    7. For godly fear 101
    8. For the love of God 103
    9. For hope 105
   10. For charity 106
   11. For chastity 107
   12. For a meek and peaceable character 108
   13. For patience 109
   14. For the mortifying of sinful desires 111
   15. For sincerity 112
   16. For a submissive spirit before God 114
   17. For increase of grace 115
   18. For inner renewal 117
   19. For God's assistance 118
   20. For a sense of God's presence 119
   21. For true devotion 120
   22. For enjoyment of God's gracious presence 120
   23. For heavenly comfort 123
   24. For heavenly-mindedness 124
   25. For greater concern for eternal realities 126
   26. For a faithful profession of Christianity 128
   27. For enthusiasm as a Christian 128
   28. For grace to serve the Lord with gladness 130
   29. For wisdom to have good relationships 131
   30. For grace to speak aright 133
   31. For perseverance to endure to the end 135
   32. For preparation and readiness to die 136

6 Epilogue 138
 (i) Introduction 138
 (ii) A converted sinner praises God 138

Preface

How we pray to God our Father through Jesus Christ our Lord reveals much of what we believe and feel about God and ourselves. Therefore a collection of written prayers based upon years of praying both in leading family prayers and alone tells us a lot about a man. Further, if he is a caring pastor, diligent student of sacred Scripture and careful observer of human experience of God then his collection of prayers will also tell us a lot about prayer, especially its content and character.

The two men responsible for the prayers in this book were known and respected by their contemporaries as prayerful pastors, preachers and teachers. They are Benjamin Jenks, whose life bridged the seventeenth and eighteenth centuries, and Charles Simeon, whose life bridged the eighteenth and nineteenth centuries. The two men never met because Jenks died some thirty-five years before Simeon was born. However, they were united in their way of understanding the Christian Faith and in their commitment to what they called "the excellency of the liturgy", the Book of Common Prayer of 1662.

Benjamin Jenks

Benjamin Jenks (1646–1724) was born during the English Civil War and he died in an age of rationalism. In his lifetime there was the ascendancy of Cromwell, the return of Charles II, the beginnings of English Nonconformity, the restoration of the Church of England (1660–62), and the rise of deism and rationalism at the turn of the century. He was the rector of Harley in Shropshire and chaplain to the Earl of Bradford: he commended a warm, rich and deep piety based soundly on the Scriptures and the Book of Common Prayer. Thus his prayers are set in this context, informed by concepts and language drawn from the Authorised Version of the Bible and the Book of Common Prayer, and set alive by a lively and sincere faith in the God and Father of our Lord Jesus Christ.

In 1697 he published primarily for his parishioners a book of prayers entitled: *Prayers and Offices of Devotion for Families and for particular Persons upon most Occasions.* It contained prayers for the whole family and for individuals within it and these prayers cover a wide spectrum of experience and conditions of life. By the time of his death the book was in its seventh edition and at the time of the French Revolution and the birth of the nineteenth century it had reached its twenty-fifth edition, proving popular in New York State as well as in Britain.

Charles Simeon

The book was "discovered" by Charles Simeon (1759–1836), Fellow of King's College, and Vicar of Holy Trinity, Cambridge, early in his ordained ministry. He came to appreciate it and later wrote that he "considered this book as an exceedingly rich treasure to the Church of God". He went on to explain that "its distinguishing excellency is, that far the greater part of the prayers appear to have been prayed and not merely written. There is a spirit of humiliation in them which is admirably suited to express the sentiments of a contrite heart. There is also a fervour of devotion in them which can scarcely fail of kindling a corresponding flame in the breasts of those who use them." He concluded by stating that it was "needless to pronounce a eulogy on a book, the value of which has been already stamped by the sale of many myriads".

However, Simeon realised that the book would have a continuing ministry in the new century if it were revised to meet the needs of people in the emerging industrial society. He saw no need for any changes in doctrine or piety/devotion; he was more concerned with the language and the need to make the sentences shorter and adapt the style. His revision of Jenks' book came out in 1808 and there were at least thirteen editions in the next fifty years. The prestige of Simeon, the leading evangelical clergyman of the time who had a profound influence upon the lives of thousands of young men, gave a new lease of life to this admirable collection of prayers and it was used widely in many Anglican and Nonconformist homes.

A modern edition

The present edition is shorter than Simeon's and this is because we felt obliged to omit some of the prayers since they reflect the social conditions and relationships of masters and servants, husbands and wives, soldiers and sailors, rulers and people, the sick and healthy, and the rich and poor of the early nineteenth century. This means that the present collection lacks the variety of intercessory and petitionary prayers of the original. However, it is rich in prayers for use by families, on the Lord's Day, for growing in grace and knowledge of our Lord Jesus Christ and other important themes.

In fact our task has not been unlike that of Simeon's in 1807–8. In sympathy with the teaching and aspirations of Jenks and Simeon, we have sought to modernise the language in order to retain the "fervour of devotion" and the "spirit of humiliation" found in the collection, making it accessible and available in the late twentieth century. This has not been easy since it is a much greater task than merely replacing "thee" and "thy" with "you" and "your"!

We hope that what we have provided will stimulate a desire in those who read and use the prayers to pray more sincerely, faithfully and humbly. They are of such a nature that they can be prayed as written or used as models for composing one's own prayers on similar themes. None of us is an expert in prayer and there is always something we can learn from others whether they live today or generations ago. Further, at a secondary level, they can also function as a statement of the practical application of Christian doctrine both in prayer and in daily vocation.

The Vicarage, Staindrop,   Peter and Vita Toon
County Durham   30 December 1989

1

PROLOGUE

(i) Introduction

The first prayer in the book is one which Benjamin Jenks composed for himself as a pastor, preacher and teacher in the parish of Harley in Shropshire. It was so easy in those days for the parson to become a country gentleman and spend his time in other pursuits than the increase of the kingdom of God. No doubt Jenks felt such temptations for he was well-connected socially; but he chose to seek to be a faithful minister of the gospel in the Established Church of England.

In a very different situation, Charles Simeon prayed the same prayer as he ministered not to country people but to young men in the University of Cambridge.

This prayer gives us confidence to read and pray the rest of the prayers in this book. By its content we know that we shall be using the prayers of godly, learned and caring men of God whose great aim in life was to glorify their Saviour. Though times have changed, the eternal God remains ever the same and we, his creatures, have the same spiritual needs as did people in earlier centuries.

(ii) A Minister's prayer

O blessed Jesus, my Lord and my God, what high honour have you given me in calling me to the office which you were pleased to take upon yourself! You came not to be

ministered unto but to minister and to preach the gospel of
the kingdom and teach the way of salvation. All glory be
to you for you have been pleased to dignify me with so high
an office.

Since you yourself as the cornerstone are to some a stone
to stumble over and a rock to be offended by, so your
messengers are to some a means unto life and to others a
means unto death. And if your wise and holy servant asked,
"Who is equal to such a task?", well may I (a weak and
sinful creature) tremble, lest those amongst whom I minister
should perish through my insufficiency or neglect and their
blood be required at my hands: yes, well may I fear, lest,
when I have shewed others the way to heaven, I myself
should be shut out!

Yet, O Lord, my life, my strength, and my Redeemer,
you have appointed me to this position: to you, therefore,
I look to qualify me for it. From the lips of children and
infants you have ordained praise, therefore magnify your
power in my weakness that I may do all things as I ought
through Christ strengthening me. O let me learn from you
what I shall teach others about you. Open my understanding, O Lord, that I may understand the Scriptures: and
enable me rightly to handle the word of truth and by sound
doctrine to encourage and convince doubters. O put such
thoughts into my mind and such words into my mouth that,
out of the abundance of my heart, my mouth may speak
to the glory of your name and to the edification of those
who hear me.

O make me wise to win souls and to be watchful over them
as one that must give an account. Let me not entangle myself
in the affairs of this life but be wholly involved in my
ministry, watching over myself and my doctrine, and
studying to present myself to God as one approved, a
workman who is thoroughly equipped for every good work.
Give me skill and conduct prudently to steer my course
through all the difficulties in my way: and give me patience
and courage to withstand all assaults and opposition which
I may have to encounter.

O my Lord, be with me to guide and help me: strengthen and succour me, now and always, in the great work in which I am involved. Give me opportunity to speak your word as I ought to speak: make me faithful, diligent and successful in my sacred calling, doing your work as a workman who need not be ashamed; may I not preach myself but Christ Jesus the Lord; and may I not seek the praise of men but the honour of my God. Yes, make me an example of all the holy duties which I urge upon others; that I may not lay upon them burdens which I myself refuse to bear; but may go before them in the ways which they are to follow; let me hold forth the Word of life in my way of life as well as in my doctrine. Let me shine with a convincing light before them, and never place an impediment in their way. Let me never make the heart of the godly sad, nor strengthen the hands of the wicked; nor give just offence to any, but let me be accepted by all as an able, useful and helpful minister. Help me to keep my body under control as my servant so that after I have preached to others I myself shall not be disqualified from receiving my heavenly prize.

You, Lord, give the increase! Command a blessing, I pray, upon all my studies and endeavours that I may not spend my strength for nothing, nor work in vain. May I make full proof of my ministry and be instrumental through your grace to convert sinners from their errors. Teach me also to build up those who are being sanctified in the most holy faith. Grant that I may both save myself and those who hear me. When I have finished my ministry may I give an account of my stewardship with joy and not with grief; and receive a crown of righteousness at your hands, not for my merits, but for the sake of your mercy. *Amen. Amen.*

2

FAMILY PRAYERS
FOR USE ON WEEKDAYS

(i) Introduction

Family Prayers were regarded as of the greatest importance
by Christian leaders from the sixteenth through to the
nineteenth centuries. A constant stream of books was
published to provide guidance and material for this daily
duty. Jenks provided seven prayers for the morning and the
same number for the evening. He intended that the father
of the family should use them to guide his own prayer at
the daily devotions. They originated in his own home and
were first published for his parishioners. Simeon commended them to families throughout Britain.

They are imbued with a deep sense of God's majesty,
holiness and righteousness and of human sinfulness and
failure. Further, they are characterised by a great confidence
in Jesus Christ as the only Mediator between sinful mankind
and God, the Father. In them are themes which are rarely
heard today — e.g. the wrath and judgement of God and
the need for godly fear in the soul. And there is a profound
sense of the reality of heaven and hell!

The prayers for mornings are basically petitions, while
those for the evenings are both petitions and intercessions.
The Lord's Prayer is recommended for use each morning
not only as a simple prayer but also as a meditative prayer.
Thus there is also provided an extended form of the Lord's
Prayer as an example of meditative praying.

(ii) Seven Morning prayers

1

O Lord, you are the God of our salvation. You are the hope of all the ends of the earth. Upon you the eyes of all are fixed. You give to everyone life, breath and all things. In you we live, and move and have our being. Upon you we continually depend for all the good that we either have, or hope for. You watch over us for good, and take care of us in our sleep, when we are incapable of caring for ourselves. Daily you renew your tender mercies to us. Every morning affords us fresh occasions for praise and thanksgiving.

You have assured us by your Word that, if we commit our affairs to you and acknowledge you in all our ways, you will establish our thoughts, and direct our path. We desire, therefore, O Lord, to put ourselves under your gracious direction and your fatherly protection. We ask for the guidance, blessing and assistance of your good Spirit to choose our inheritance for us, and to make use of us, and of all that concerns us, to the glory of your name.

O Lord, do not withdraw your tender mercies from us. Do not take away the comforts of your presence or the assistance of your Spirit because of our many abuses of your grace and goodness. Never punish our past sins by giving us over to the love and power of our sins. Give us truly penitent hearts, and grant us your merciful discharge from all the guilt that lies upon us. Further, grant us, O good God, the delightful sense of your acceptance of us in the Son of your love, that our souls may bless you, and all that is within us may praise your holy name.

O that we may find the joy of the Lord to be our strength! That we may be strengthened by it against all our sins, especially the sins to which we are most addicted, and from which we are most in danger. Make us also more ready to do every good work, and better disposed for all the duties which we owe to you, our neighbour and ourselves. Grant that in these tasks we may so exercise ourselves as to have always a conscience void of offence towards God and towards fellow human beings. O help us to walk cautiously, not foolishly but wisely, carefully redeeming the time that we have lost, and putting to good use all opportunities you give us to experience your grace.

While we are upon earth give us all things necessary and convenient for our present pilgrimage. Sanctify to us all our enjoyments and all our activities in the world. Let our crosses as well as our comforts and everything which happens to us enhance your glory, until, through the merits of your Son and the multitude of your mercies, we are conducted safely to be ever with the Lord. Amidst all our other affairs in this world let us never forget or neglect the one thing that is necessary. May it be our principal care so to conduct ourselves every day, that we may give our account with joy on the great day of your appearing.

O gracious Father, keep us we beseech you, this day in your fear and favour. Help us to live to your honour and glory. If you do not guide us we shall run into errors. If you do not preserve us we shall fall into dangers. Let your good providence be our defence and security and let your Holy Spirit be our guide and counsellor in all our ways. Grant that we may do those things which are agreeable to your will, and acceptable in your sight, through Jesus Christ, in whose sacred name and words, we close our imperfect petitions:

Our Father . . .

Let your grace, O Lord Jesus Christ, your love, O heavenly Father, and your comforting fellowship, O Holy Spirit, be with us and with all the people of God, this day and for evermore. *Amen.*

2

O Lord, you are our God and we ought to serve you with all the abilities with which you have blessed us. We are bound, by all the obligations of your commandments and by all the endearments of your love, to be faithful in the covenant of our God and to abound in the work of the Lord. We desire to humble ourselves before you because our lives have been so unserviceable to you and so full of provocation against you. The dishonour we have done you, O Lord, has much exceeded all our services. We have lived to ourselves rather than to you. We have served our own lusts and pleasures more than your holy, blessed will. We have disbelieved your truths, disobeyed your commands and disregarded your promises and threats! We have resisted and defeated all the gracious methods which you have used to reclaim us from our evil ways and to bring us to yourself.

We have sinned against you, our God, and done infinite wrong and damage to our own souls. By our sins we have spoiled and destroyed ourselves. But it is not in us, O Lord, to recover and save ourselves. In you, O Heavenly Father, in you alone, is all our help. You have made Jesus a high priest forever so that he is able to save completely those who come to you through him. Through him you have encouraged us to come boldly to the throne of grace, that we may obtain mercy and find grace to help in every time of need. In him, therefore, we beg, O Lord, that you will be reconciled to us, and make yourself known to us as a Father of mercies, and a God of all comfort.

For his sake, enable us also, we pray, to conduct ourselves as becomes the children of God, and the members and followers of Christ. O put such principles of grace and holiness into our hearts which will make us hate all iniquity and abhor every false way. Put your Spirit within us, and cause us to walk in your statutes, to keep your directives and to do them. Do not merely lay your commands upon us but be pleased, O Lord, to enable us to perform them.

So give us life by your grace that we may make it our meat and drink to do your will. May we observe your commandments with enlarged hearts. Make our services acceptable to you while we live and our souls ready for you when we die. As long as we are in this world keep us, O

Lord our God, from the evil of it and from the snares and dangers to which you know we are continually exposed. Make a passage for us through all the changes, troubles and temptations of this mortal life, and bring us finally to the unchangeable glories and blessedness of the eternal world.

Be merciful to us, good Lord, and bless us, and keep us this day in all our ways. Let us take nothing in hand which is not warranted by your Word. O let us be in the fear of the Lord all the day long. Let your fear be ever before our eyes to restrain us from the things which are displeasing to you and destructive to our own souls. Let your love abound in our hearts, and sweetly and powerfully constrain us to perform whatever is acceptable in your sight, through him who has loved and redeemed us, even the Lord our righteousness in whose blessed name and words we continue praying:

Our Father . . .

The blessing of God almighty, Father, Son, and Holy Spirit, be with us, and with all who belong to us, this day and for evermore. *Amen.*

3

O Lord God, merciful and gracious, longsuffering, and abundant in goodness and truth! You show mercy to thousands. You pardon iniquity, transgression and sin. You do not remain angry for ever, because you delight in mercy. How excellent is your loving-kindness, O God! Therefore human beings take refuge in the shadow of your wings, and we continue to look up to your bountiful hand from which we have received all our good things.

O Lord our God, be pleased to look down mercifully upon us, and be gracious and favourable to us as you have always been to those who love your name. O look not upon the inbred sin of our human nature nor on the sins of our hearts and lives, which are more than we can remember and greater than we can express. Behold, we are unworthy; we are exceeding guilty. We acknowledge that it is because you are merciful and that your compassion does not fail that we are not consumed.

But look upon us in mercy, through the merits and mediation of your Son, our Saviour. Pity us for his sake who did no sin, and was manifested to take away our sins. By him let us have access to your gracious Majesty. For his sake bestow upon us the blessings which we so greatly need. We believe that you have treasured up in him an infinite fulness of all that we can ever want or wish. O that we may all receive out of his fulness grace sufficient for our every need!

O Father, let us receive from him those gifts which he is now empowered and commissioned to bestow, those gifts which he purchased by his blood, and which are the necessary means of our salvation. Pour down upon us the abundance of your grace. Accept and justify our persons. Renew and sanctify our souls. So transform us into your image that we may be worthy partakers of the inheritance of your saints in light.

Teach us, O Lord our God, to use this world without abusing it, and to enjoy the things of it without allowing them to engross our affections. Whatever we have of the world let it be sanctified to us by the Word of God and prayer. O Lord, our heavenly Father, leave us not destitute of those things that accompany salvation. Adorn our souls with all the graces of your Holy Spirit that we may glorify you in all things, and that our conversation may be such as adorns the Gospel of Christ.

Help us, O gracious Lord, in the whole of our duty to you, our God, and also in the discharge of all related duties which we owe to our fellow human beings, whether superiors, equals or inferiors. Enable us to behave wisely towards them which are outside and kindly towards them that are within. Let us never cast a stumbling-block in the way of others, nor cause your holy name to be blasphemed through our misconduct. Let us pass the time of our pilgrimage here in godly fear so that, having glorified you on earth, we may be glorified by you in the great day of our Lord Jesus Christ.

Now that you have renewed your mercies to us this morning, help us, gracious God, to renew our desires and endeavours to serve and honour you. Restrain us from the evils and follies into which we are prone to fall. Make us eager to do the tasks and duties which we are averse to perform. Grant that we may think, speak and act as befits saints, ever remembering that we are bought with the precious blood of Christ and ever striving to live unto him, who died for us and rose again, to whom with the Father and the Holy Spirit be glory and honour, world without end.

Our Father . . .

4

O Lord God you hear prayer, and are near to all who call upon you in truth. We are moved by our own necessities, and encouraged by your daily mercies, to renew our petitions at the throne of your grace. We ask you, who mould human hearts, to prepare our hearts, that we may now come into your holy presence and call upon your blessed name acceptably. Pour upon us the Spirit of grace and of supplication. Let your good Spirit help our weaknesses. Teach us to ask such things and in such a way which will be most advantageous to our souls.

Behold! We, who are but as poor worms, and sinful dust and ashes, have taken upon us to speak unto you, the sovereign Majesty of heaven and earth. We are justly afraid lest our great and manifold sins should have provoked you to hide your face from us and to cut us off from your loving-kindness in displeasure. We know that we have acted wickedly in not listening to the calls of your Word, or yielding to the motions of your Spirit. Our iniquities are increased over our heads; our transgression is grown up even unto heaven and our sins are a painful burden, too heavy for us to bear. If you, O Lord, should enter into judgement with us we could not defend ourselves on one count out of a thousand. We must place our hands over our mouths, and plead guilty before you and place our dependence wholly upon your mercy.

O God, be merciful to us, miserable sinners. For the sake of him whom you have exalted to be a Prince and a Saviour to give repentance to your people and forgiveness of sins, be merciful to us, we pray. Heal our souls that have greatly sinned against you. Heal our backslidings, renew us to repentance and establish our walk in your holy ways. Let us not be so wavering and so prone to backsliding. Let us never revolt against you and return to folly after you have spoken peace to us. May we go on conquering and to conquer all the enemies of our souls until every obstacle to our salvation is overcome, and Satan himself is bruised under our feet.

O God of all grace, bring such thoughts to our minds and lay such considerations upon our hearts as you know will effectively keep us from iniquity, and prevail with us to do your will. Put your fear into our hearts that we may not depart from you anymore. Preserve us holy and unblamable unto the coming of our Lord Jesus Christ. In the meantime sanctify to us all the ordering of your providence and bless us in every condition and relation of life. Make us humble in an high position or contented with a low one; nor ever let us forget that the care of our souls is the one thing that is needed. O make us mindful of this, that we may follow unceasingly those things which shall bring us peace at the last.

Direct us, and all that concerns us, we beseech you, to the glory of your name. Keep us at all times, and in all places and companies, from the evil of sin, and from all other evils to which the greatness of our sins has made us liable. Take, O heavenly Father, gracious charge and rule over us this day. So guide us by your counsel that hereafter you may receive us to glory. All this we ask through your tender mercies and our Saviour's abundant merits, in whose own words we ask all things needful for ourselves and others at your hands:

Our Father . . .

5

O Lord our God! Your name is most excellent in all the earth. You have set up your glory above the heavens and you are worthy to be celebrated with everlasting praises of men and angels. You have created all things, and for your pleasure they are, and were created. Your hands, O Lord, have made us and moulded us. You have breathed into us the breath of life. You sustain our souls in life, and give us every good thing that makes our lives a blessing and a comfort to us. You have formed us for yourself that we should show forth your praise and live to your glory as we continually rely upon your bounty.

O Lord our God, we have in no respect glorified you as we ought. Instead we have greatly dishonoured you in the whole course of our lives! Time after time we have forgotten you, the gracious giver of all our good things, and the One who is always mindful of us. O how soon have we become weary of serving you, while you are never weary of doing good to us! We have not only neglected your work, but have been disobedient to your Word and have followed after our own foolish lusts, which might have drowned us in destruction and complete ruin, long ago.

For these failings we desire to pour out our hearts, and to humble our sinful selves here before you. For the sake of your mercy in Christ Jesus, which has moved you to spare us for so long and to do so much for us already, we entreat you to pity us. Give us repentant hearts and pardon us for all our past offences, whether in omitting our duty, or failing in it, or acting contrary to it. For your dear Son's sake absolve us thoroughly from the guilt of all our sins.

Strengthen us, good Lord, with power by your Spirit in our spirits that we may be more watchful against temptation, and more victorious over our inner corruptions. O destroy in us every sinful inclination, every evil habit, every rebellious motion that exalts itself against the knowledge of God and of Christ Jesus, our Lord. Increase and confirm in us, more and more, the graces of your Holy Spirit, especially those which you know to be most lacking in us, and most necessary for us.

Fill us with the knowledge of your will, with faith in your promises and with the fear and love of your holy name. Give us whatsoever shall make our lives more comfortable to ourselves, more profitable to others and more honourable to you, our God. Whatever be our concerns at this present time, may we still be found in the way of our duty, fearing God and working righteousness. May we make sure of our union with Christ, the great Saviour of the world that, when all earthly help shall fail us, you may care for us and be the strength of our hearts, and our portion for ever.

Day by day we magnify you, O Lord, for you are making every day a further addition to your mercies. We bless you for our last night's preservation and protection, and for the rest and refreshment which you have given us in it. O cause us to hear your loving-kindness in the morning, for in you do we trust. Cause us to know the way in which we shall go, for we lift up our souls to you. Cast us not away from your presence. Take not your Holy Spirit from us. Direct all our ways to please you, our God, that you may crown us with blessing and good success.

Help us to see your power, to recognise your presence, to admire your wisdom and to love your goodness in all your creatures. By all the provisions of your providence draw us still nearer to yourself, the blessed Creator of every comfort. Let our meditations of God be sweet as well as frequent, that, delighting ourselves in the Lord, we may obtain the desire of our hearts. We ask such mercy and grace for ourselves, for our families and your elect everywhere, in our great Mediator's model prayer:

Our Father . . .

6

We present ourselves this morning before your glorious Majesty, most blessed Lord God, desiring to pay you that tribute, homage and service, of prayer and praise, which is so justly due to you. We desire to approach you in such a manner, that you may mercifully accept both us and our services, at the hands of Jesus Christ. In his great name we come to you at your command, and worship at your footstool. In his name we implore your pardon. We earnestly ask you to give us an increase of your grace, and fresh tokens of your love.

We are not worthy indeed that you should take notice of us, or be entreated by us, but worthy is the Lamb that was slain to take away the sins of the world. Worthy is the Lamb, that you should for his sake do more for us than we can ask or even think. He fulfilled those holy laws which we have broken and he perfectly satisfied divine justice for all our transgressions of them. In him you are a God who is gracious and merciful, slow to anger and of great kindness even to the chief of sinners. In him you are reconciled to those who deserve nothing but to be forsaken and abhorred by you. We acknowledge that we ought to be thoroughly ashamed. Our sins have been so multiplied, that we might well expect your wrath and judgement. If you should be zealous to mark what we have done erroneously and defectively, we could not escape the curses of your holy law.

But, O gracious Father, do not count what we have done against your Majesty. Instead reckon what our blessed Saviour has done for our souls. Consider not what we have made ourselves, but what you made of Christ to us. May Christ be to every one of us (what he is to all your faithful people) wisdom and righteousness, and sanctification and redemption! Let his precious blood cleanse us from all our sins and let the grace of your Holy Spirit renew and sanctify our souls.

Righteous Father, subdue, we pray you, our iniquities,

and mortify our lusts. Inspire us to do all the duties of your holy service, and enable us to perform them with profit and delight. Let not sin reign in our mortal bodies, that we should obey its lusts. Let there be no sin in us which is not felt and hated, bewailed and resisted by us. Let us keep our own hearts open to you, the searcher of them, and let all our ways be pleasing in your sight.

O teach us to know you, our God, and enable us to do your will as we ought to do. Give us hearts to fear you and to love you. Cause us to trust in you and to cling with faithfulness to you. Let no temptations draw us, nor any sorrows drive us, from you. Let all your dealings with us be received as messengers of your love to our souls. Let all your handling of us bring us nearer to your blessed self, and make us fitter for your heavenly kingdom.

Enliven us, O Lord, in our dullness. Instead of dishonouring you by our lifeless and listless services, may we abound in your work, and be fervent in spirit, always serving the Lord. Make us also faithful in all our relationships with our neighbours. Make us ready to do good, and to bear evil. Make us just and kind, merciful and meek, peaceable and patient, sober and temperate, humble and self-denying, inoffensive and exemplary in our conduct. By so glorifying you here upon earth may we at our departure be received into the joy of our Lord, and be for ever glorified in your heavenly kingdom.

You have kept us alive to this day, and have refreshed us during the night season; renew, we pray, your mercy to us together with this morning's light. You call forth songs of joy where morning dawns and evening fades, and so we ask that you will make your face to shine upon us and make us glad with the tokens of your love. As you are always present with us, make us ever aware of your presence, that we may duly remember you in all our ways and wisely conduct ourselves in all our affairs.

Be with us, good Lord, at our going out and our coming in. Let your grace follow us this day, and all the days of our life. O never leave us, and never, never forsake us but' be our guide unto death. In death comfort us, and after death be our everlasting portion. O hear us from heaven, your dwelling-place. Do more for us than we are worthy to expect at your hands for Jesus's sake, who alone is worthy, and in whose comprehensive words we sum up all our desires:

Our Father . . .

7

O Lord God Almighty, you are the sovereign Majesty of heaven and earth, against whom all our sins have been committed, and by whom alone they can be pardoned! There is none but you by whom our iniquities can be forgiven, our souls be sanctified, and our necessities supplied. But you are able and also ready to hear and help, to bless and save your people that call upon you. You delight to show mercy, and love the opportunities for glorifying your compassion.

Therefore, we come to you, O Lord, begging that mercy, which you know we deeply desire, and that grace to help us in this time of our need. We ask this for the sake of your infinitely beloved Son, who alone is worthy, and in whose precious blood is all our trust.

We are unclean, Lord, we are unclean! You may well abhor our guilty souls but look upon us in the Son of your love. Prepare us for the mercies which you have treasured up for us in him. Make us feel the burden and the bitterness of our sins. Never let us attempt to cover and conceal them lest they find us out at the last and overwhelm us with shame and misery.

Holy Father, carry on with power your great work within us, even the work of faith, and the sanctification of our souls. Enliven us, O Lord our God, and stir us up to do your work. Assist us in the performance of all our duties, which of ourselves you know we are unable to accomplish. Work in us to will and to do of your good pleasure.

Establish the things, O God, which you have already done for us, and go on to work mightily upon our hearts by your grace until our souls are fitted for the enjoyment of your glory.

Gracious Lord, your mercies are fresh and new to us every morning. We have laid down and slept and awaked again because you have sustained us. You have kept us from the terrors of the night and from all evil accidents so that we are once more risen in peace and safety. Glory be to you, O God of our salvation, who are still mindful of us, and so merciful unto us.

Go on, we pray you, to be good to us this day and teach us how to conduct ourselves aright, and to order our affairs to your glory. O direct our undertakings, and prosper our endeavours. Rule our hearts in your fear and love, and keep us living to your praise and honour. Behold, we commit ourselves to you, and shelter ourselves under the shadow of your wings. Keep us from evil, and help us to do that which is good and pleasing to our God through Jesus Christ. Give us, O Lord, all that we have asked as we should, and forgive us all that we have asked wrongly. Bestow on us all things needful which we should have asked: and which we continue to ask in the comprehensive words of your dear Son:

Our Father . . .

(iii) Seven Evening prayers

1

O Lord our God, you are infinitely great and infinitely good. Your glory is above all our thoughts, and your mercies are more than can be numbered. We have so much cause to admire and bless and praise you for making us the objects of your love and the living monuments of your goodness. When we survey your glorious perfections, especially as they shine forth in the person of Jesus Christ, we are encouraged to come unto you and we are emboldened to call you Father. Though we have great and many sins to confess yet do we look up with confidence, trusting that you will pardon them and give us power from on high to mortify and subdue them.

You created us, O Lord, after your own blessed image, in a holy and happy state; but we have made ourselves abject and miserable. We are no longer upright; we have become averse to good, and prone to evil. Yes, so full are we of all iniquity, that we are a mystery to ourselves. We wonder at the sinfulness of our own hearts, and are astonished that you have not cut us off in anger, and shut us up under final despair of mercy long ago.

You have declared your willingness to be reconciled even to your enemies. You have sent your only Son into the world for this very end. You have sent him, that all might believe in him and that whosoever believes in him should not perish but have everlasting life. O Lord, we believe; help our unbelief. Give us true repentance towards God, and right faith in our Lord Jesus Christ that we may be of the number of those who repent and believe in order to save their souls.

Save us, good Lord, from the love and the ways of this present evil world, and from every self-destroying route which we are tempted to follow. Make for us a path to escape out of all the snares of temptation with which we have been entangled. Let us so experience the bitterness of sin and the excellence of your ways, that we may disregard both the attractions and discouragements of this world. Establish, strengthen, and secure us, O Lord, that going forth in your strength we may please you in faithfully doing your will and by continuing in your fear to our lives' end.

While we plead for your mercy for ourselves, we would humbly implore your blessing, O Lord, on all those whom we ought to remember in our prayers. O bring near to yourself all those that are yet afar off, and reveal the sweetness of your knowledge in every place. Let such as sit in darkness and the shadow of death behold the light of your truth and the joy of your salvation. Grant that all who name the name of Christ may depart from iniquity, and so live up to their profession as to give no just occasion for your enemies to blaspheme! Let it be the ambition of all your people to adorn the doctrine of God our Saviour in all things, and to put to silence the ignorance of foolish men by well doing.

Be gracious and favourable, O Lord, to your Church, and especially to that part of it which you have planted in this nation. Arise O God, and plead your own cause, and maintain your holy religion which you have so long established amongst us. Let not the enemies of your Church ever have cause to say that they have prevailed against your people. Let those who embrace your cause and stand up for the defence of your truth go on and prosper. May they ever have cause to say, "The Lord be magnified who has pleasure in the prosperity of his servants."

Bless with the choicest of your blessings the Queen whom you have put in authority over us. Protect her person, direct her councils, and prosper all her endeavours for the peace and welfare of her dominions. Give to all magistrates wisdom and courage to defend your truth, and to do right to all. Make all ministers to be examples to the flock, in all righteousness and holiness of living. Establish all of us to be an holy people to yourself. Grant us one heart, and one way, that we may fear you for ever, for our own good and that of our children after us.

Comfort all who lack the comforts which we enjoy and relieve the needs of all your afflicted people throughout the world. Remember all our friends and benefactors, our kindred after the flesh, and all who are near and dear to us. Remember them with the favour which you bear to your people. Make them, O Lord, such as you would have them be so that you will mercifully accept them into your favour here, and to your kingdom hereafter. Look also upon our enemies. Forgive them and turn their hearts. Enable us to forgive them as we hope for forgiveness at your hands. Enable us to overcome their evil with good and so please you in all our ways, that you may make our enemies to be at peace with us.

Hear us, O God of the spirits of all flesh. Hear us both for ourselves and others. Above all hear the Son of your love pleading for us at your right hand. Hear his all-prevailing intercessions for us, and for all the members of his mystical body. To him we commit our cause, and to you through him; trusting in your tender mercy, and ascribing to him, to you and to your blessed Spirit all possible honour, might, majesty, and dominion, both now and forever. *Amen.*

2

Our ever blessed and most precious God! You are the Lord and giver of our lives and of all the blessings we enjoy. To you we owe ourselves, and all that we are capable of rendering to you. For by you, O Lord, we were created. Through your good providence we have been spared and provided for unto this present time. From you, our God, comes all our help and in you rests all our hope. You are the bountiful giver of all the good that our souls desire, and the merciful withholder of all the evil that our sins deserve.

We acknowledge your great and daily goodness to us, and our own exceeding unworthiness of the least of all your mercies. We are truly ashamed of ourselves, that we have so little improved, and so greatly abused all your patience with us and all the various instances of your bounty to us. We confess it to be an odious aggravation of our offences that we have done so much against you after all the great things you have done for us.

We desire to be humbled, O Lord, for our offences. We plead your gracious favour in Christ Jesus for the pardon of them. Forgive us we pray you (for his sake) all the sins which we have ever committed against you, and absolve us from all the evil of which we now stand guilty before you. Being justified by faith, let us have peace with God through Jesus Christ.

We pray that you will be to us a Father of mercies, and a God of consolation. We pray that you will make us followers of God, as dear children, ever jealous over our hearts and watchful over our ways. May we continually fear to offend you and always endeavour to please you. Enable us to keep our hearts with all diligence that they may never be hardened through the deceitfulness of sin.

You know, O Lord, our weakness and our danger. You know how unable we are of ourselves to resist the smallest temptation while we are continually exposed to the assaults of our subtle enemy, to the allurements of an ensnaring world, and to the corruptions of our own treacherous hearts. We pray therefore, good Lord, that you will arm us with the whole armour of God, and uphold us with your free Spirit and evermore watch over us for good. In the times of our sorest trials especially let us experience the strongest assistance of your heavenly grace, that we may never fall a prey to those deadly enemies that seek to devour us.

Teach us, O God, to know the day of grace, and the time of our visitation and to see the things of our peace, before they are hidden from our eyes. While we have time, enable us to use it fruitfully for those great ends for which you are pleased to continue it to us. Let us not neglect that precious talent, which you have given us, but employ it with all diligence and attention for the securing of our eternal welfare.

Seeing you are pleased to sustain our souls in life, and to make us find and feel by every day's experience how abundantly gracious and merciful you are, give us hearts more aware of your love. May they be more touched with your mercy and more thankful for those continued favours which you are pleased to grant to us. Help us to show forth your praise not only by speaking good of your name but by ordering our conversation aright and by adorning the gospel of God our Saviour in all we do.

Now, most merciful Father, we humbly commend ourselves and all that we have to your care and protection. We beseech you for your dear Son's sake to preserve and defend, to bless and keep us, both in soul and body. We know that by reason of our weakness and wickedness we are exposed to many and great dangers but we commit ourselves to you, trusting that you will sustain us.

Be with us through the night season, and grant us comfortable rest that our frail nature may be refreshed and our decayed strength renewed. May we rise again better fitted for the duties of the following day, if you should be pleased to add another day to our lives. As you daily multiply your mercies to us, be pleased to increase our repentance, and to renew us daily after your image. May every day not only bring us nearer to your kingdom, but make us fitter for the enjoyment of that glory which you have prepared for them that love you.

Accept these our prayers, most gracious and merciful Lord God. For all the good things we have received, or at present enjoy, or hope for in the future from your bountiful hands, enable us to render our grateful thanks. Let it be our employment now, as we hope it shall be hereafter, abundantly to utter the memory of your great goodness, and to sing of your praise without ceasing. *Amen and Amen.*

3

O Lord, you are our gracious God, our chief good, and our most merciful Father in Christ Jesus. In his great name, and through his prevailing mediation, we are encouraged to present ourselves and our prayers before you. It is a great privilege, which we must acknowledge ourselves utterly unworthy to enjoy, that you should admit us into your service as well as into fellowship with your blessed self.

We do not presume to appear in the presence of your glorious Majesty in our own name or trusting in any righteousness of our own. We are conscious of so much guilt, as might make us tremble for fear of your judgements; but we come in the name and mediation of your dear Son, who has fully satisfied your justice for our sins, and continually intercedes for us at your right hand. You love him infinitely above all, and delight to honour him in sparing and accepting the most unworthy sinners upon his account.

O deliver us, most gracious Lord, for his sake, from all transgressions for which our hearts condemn us. Deliver us from all which you (who are greater than our hearts) know us to be guilty. Seal to us a full pardon in his most precious blood which speaks better things on our behalf than we are able to speak for ourselves.

Our past lives were lived to ourselves and served our own lusts and pleasures. Put an end to all our presumptuous and treacherous dealings. Grant us new and contrite hearts, that we may tremble at your presence and hate and abandon every evil way. Hold fast, O blessed Lord, the deepest thoughts of our minds, the choicest affections of our hearts, and the inner tendency and activity of our souls. O let us delight in attending upon you and in communion with you. Do not let the vanities of this world ever divert us from your service, or interrupt our enjoyment of your presence.

Hear us, O Lord, for ourselves, and let our petitions also ascend before you on behalf of all people. Send your Word and the means of grace to those who are destitute of them. Make them effective and a delight to those who now enjoy them. Convert the unconverted, and perfect your good work where you have begun it. Provide a check to all irreverence and ungodliness so that presumptuous sinners may be ashamed, and that the wickedness of the wicked may come to an end.

O make your Church to increase and flourish and your servants to prevail and rejoice. Be gracious and favourable to this our native land, to the head and governors of it, and to all the inhabitants. Rule all our rulers, counsel our counsellors, teach all our teachers, and order all public affairs to the glory of your name and to the welfare of our Church and state.

Turn from us, good Lord, the judgements which we feel or fear. Continue to us the many temporal and spiritual advantages which through your favour we enjoy. Notwithstanding all the devices of our enemies and all the despicable provocations of our sins, continue to be our reconciled God, and let us be your happy and peculiar people.

Look down, O Gracious Father, on all the sons and daughters of affliction. Mercifully view them under the pressure of their troubles, and think thoughts of pity and compassion towards them. O sanctify your fatherly corrections to them, support them under their various burdens and in your good time deliver them from the furnace into which they are cast.

Be gracious to all our friends and neighbours, reward our benefactors and bless our relations with the choicest of your blessings. Bless also our enemies and reconcile them both to us and to yourself. Dwell in all the habitations which you have made houses of prayer and with all the families who call upon your name.

Let your heavenly blessings and your saving grace descend and rest upon this family. O guide us and keep us. Make us wise and faithful in our duty and prosperous in all our lawful undertakings. Bless all our present circumstances and fit us for whatever changes we may be called to experience. O teach us how to want and how to abound. Whether we are in a prosperous or suffering condition secure our hearts to yourself and make us upright before you.

Now, O Lord, be pleased to accept our evening sacrifice of praise and thanksgiving. We would glorify you, the Father of mercies and the fountain of all goodness, for the mercies of the day past, and for the goodness that has followed us all the days of our life. Our lives have been filled with your mercies, and you have abounded towards us in loving-kindness. Infinite has been the variety of the sweet and comfortable blessings with which you have showered us. You have passed by our innumerable sins as though you had not seen them, and you are still surrounding us with mercies on every side.

Imprint and preserve upon our hearts a lively and grateful sense of your kindness to us. Let our souls bless you. Let all that is within us praise your holy name. Let us give you thanks from the depth of our hearts, and praise our God whilst we have our being. Your patience with us, your care over us, and your continual mercy to us, demand our incessant praise. To you, therefore, our heavenly Father, let all thanks and praise and love and obedience and honour and glory be rendered by us, and by all the people of God, henceforth and for evermore. *Amen.*

4

O Lord, the infinite, incomprehensible God, who were before all, are above all, and will forever be the same! You have heaven for your throne and the earth for your footstool. You are present here and everywhere. You are thoroughly acquainted with all our ways. You search our hearts and keep us in check. You know the dulness and hardness, the vanity and deceitfulness of our hearts. You see how difficult we find it to bring our souls into an holy frame and to keep them in a state fit to attend upon your heavenly Majesty.

We were born in sin and in sin we have lived. Daily we have added sin to sin, and have made ourselves children of wrath more by practice than we were by nature. Every day of our lives we have transgressed your laws, abused your mercies, tempted your patience, despised your goodness and offended you more, even though you showed forbearance to us. We have made the very abundance of your grace an encouragement to continue in our sins.

O God, we have so greatly provoked you! What must we not expect if you should enter into judgement with us? How justly might you withdraw your tender mercies from us and pour upon us your wrath and indignation to the uttermost. How justly might you leave us to feel what an evil and bitter thing it is to trespass against you. And how justly might you cast us into that place of torment, where there is weeping and wailing and gnashing of teeth, and from where there is no redemption!

You are a God of wonderful patience to bear with sinners. You are a God of infinite goodness and mercy to forgive them when they are truly penitent. You have said that if the wicked forsake his way and the unrighteous man his thoughts and return to the Lord, you will have mercy upon him and abundantly pardon. We humbly ask, therefore, that you will be graciously pleased to stretch forth your powerful hand and to loose the chains of sin with which we are tied and bound. Let it be your good pleasure to deliver us from every weight of sin and from every yoke of bondage. Let our souls be fitted to serve you with that sincerity and readiness and gladness which you require of your people. O help us so to see and feel, so to hate and bewail, so to confess and forsake our sins, that we may have a well grounded hope of your forgiveness and a comfortable persuasion that you have accepted us in the Son of your love.

For his sake, grant us, O Lord, an increase of your grace and such assistance of your Holy Spirit as may enable us to mortify our sins and fit us for all the duties of your service. Make us, O God, to serve you sincerely without hypocrisy, cheerfully without dulness, universally without partiality, constantly without falling away, or being weary of well doing. You are not weary in doing us good: let us be never weary in doing you good service. As you have pleasure in the prosperity of your servants, so let us take pleasure in the service of our Lord and abound in your work and in your love and praise for evermore.

O fill us with all that is lacking, reform whatever is amiss in us and perfect that which concerns us. Make us such in our hearts and in our lives that we may obtain peace in our souls and be made partakers of your heavenly glory. Be pleased to grant us now (out of the riches of your grace) the pleasing sense of your gracious acceptance of us and of your merciful intentions towards us. O speak peace to our consciences and say to each of our souls, "I am your salvation", so that we may look upon you as our reconciled God and Father in Christ Jesus.

In his great name and through his prevailing mediation

we enlarge our petitions on behalf of the whole race of mankind. O that all people everywhere may repent and turn unto the Lord, and see the salvation of our God. Teach us to know the meaning of your divine providence and help us to improve through all your dealings with us. O turn all our hearts to you as the heart of one man. Reform all our lives according to the holy pattern and precepts of our Lord. Cause your anger towards us to cease and continue still to take charge of us and never leave nor forsake us.

Bless abundantly Her Majesty the Queen, who now sways the sceptre of these realms. O Lord, preserve her life, prolong her days, and prosper her government. Give her the hearts of her subjects and subdue her enemies before her. Make her a cause of rejoicing for your people and a terror only to evil doers. Let her continue to be a zealous defender of the faith, a promoter of your fear, and an assertor of our rights, that under her shadow we may be in peace and safety, enjoying the liberty of the gospel and the free profession of your holy religion.

Grant unto all magistrates and ministers continual supplies of your Holy Spirit for the conscientious and peaceful discharge of their various duties. Bring all our neighbours near to yourself. Be a friend to all our friends, a father to the fatherless, a husband to the widow, a refuge to the oppressed, a physician to the sick, a helper to the friendless, and a God of consolation to the distressed and sorrowful, whatever be their trouble and affliction. Bless to us whatever you are pleased to allot us, and everything that befalls us. Make all things to work for our true good, to build us up in your grace and to help us onwards to your glory.

As you have been good and kind to us in days past and throughout our whole lives (for which we desire, O Lord, humbly and thankfully to adore your name) so we ask that we may experience the continuance of your goodness to us and of your fatherly care over us this present night. O preserve and defend, bless and keep us, that no evil may befall us, nor any plague come near our dwelling. Give us sleep and rest to refresh and strengthen us for your service and for the performance of all our duties. Prepare us, O Lord, for our last sleep in death, and for that great account that we must give at the judgement-seat of Christ. Instruct and assist us in that great work of preparation for our everlasting state that we may (in this our only time of preparation) finish the great work which you have given us to do. Before the night of death overtake us in which we cannot work, grant that whenever you shall be pleased to give us the summons of death, we may find nothing to do but to die and cheerfully to resign our spirits into your gracious hands.

Hear us, we beseech you, through the riches of your grace and the worthiness of your dear Son, in whose merits alone we trust. To him, to you and to the Holy Spirit, the one God of our salvation, be all praise and honour and glory ascribed by us and by all your people from this time forth and for evermore. *Amen.*

5

O Lord, we desire to seek your face and to wait upon you in the duties of your worship. We ask for your gracious favour that we may be enabled to call upon you with our whole hearts. To whom should we make our petitions but unto you the Father of mercies, and the fountain of all goodness, who are able to do exceeding abundantly even above all that we can ask or think. You have declared your willingness to be petitioned by us and your readiness to hear and help us.

O let our prayer be now set before you as incense, and the lifting up of our hands be as the evening sacrifice, pleasing to you, our God, in the Son of your love. It is in his blessed name alone that we have encouragement to approach you, and boldness to ask of you those things which you know to be needful and expedient for us.

There is in ourselves no good thing to recommend us to your favour but rather a proneness to everything which is displeasing to your Majesty, and destructive to our souls.

We are even by nature children of wrath and the sinful offspring of rebellious parents. Ever since we began to act we have been daily trespassing against you and adding to the heavy score of our offences.

There is nothing in us, O Lord, but what may well provoke you to reject us; but, there is enough in your beloved Son to obtain for us the pardon of our sins and peace with you. You did make him to be sin for us, that we might be made the righteousness of God in him, and that we might be saved by his merits when we could not be saved by any merit of our own works. O see our sins punished in him, even in him who was wounded for our transgressions, and bruised for our iniquities. As the chastisement of our peace was upon him, so let the merit of his righteousness be on us and by his stripes let our souls be healed.

Nor do we only beg pardon of our sins, but also for power against them and grace sufficient for us to break off committing them. We long to walk more acceptably before you in all the duties of righteousness and holiness which your Word has prescribed to us. O never allow us to be tempted above what we are able to bear but make our temptations less or your grace in us more sufficient to resist them. May no iniquities prevail against us nor any arrogant sin have dominion over us. Make us conform more to the pattern and the precepts of our blessed Saviour. Transform us more into his holy image and likeness. May we not dishonour his religion nor cause the way of truth to be evil spoken of. Make our light to shine before men to the glory of our heavenly Father and to the edification of those amongst whom we dwell.

Seeing that the time of our abode in this transitory world is so very short and uncertain and that after our departure we have an everlasting state where we must be happy or miserable for ever, O let us not set up our rest in this world as if we were at home upon earth. Neither allow us to flatter ourselves with the hopes of a long enjoyment of these things which perish in our use of them. May we wait all the days of our appointed time till our change comes, and live not only in expectation of it, but in the daily and serious preparation for it. May we learn that to live is Christ and to die is gain, that in life and death we may be always yours, safe in your hands, and acceptable in your sight.

Together with our own wants, we commend to your mercy O God, the needs and distress of all our brethren throughout the world. O enlighten the ignorant, enliven the careless, awaken the secure, establish the wavering and comfort the dejected. Bring all to the knowledge of your truth and to a cheerful obedience to your holy will so that they may attain to the blessed hope of your glory and the eternal salvation of their immortal souls.

We pray for the Queen, for all our magistrates and ministers, for all our friends and relations, for all workers, and for all the afflicted throughout the world. More especially we pray for those whose happiness and salvation we have particular concern. Do for us and for them as you know best, and as is most needful and expedient, for your own mercy's sake in Christ Jesus.

As we pray to you for what we want, so we desire to praise you for all that we have received at your hands. Blessed be your name, O Lord, that we have any thing, yes, that we have so many things for which to bless and praise you. O what shall we render to the Lord for all his benefits? Dear Lord, let not our hearts be shut or decreased towards you, whose hand is every day open to us. Possess and enlarge these hearts of ours with more love and greater thankfulness to you that we may both give thanks and glorify your name for evermore.

Now that the night is upon us and we are ready to take our rest, we commit ourselves to your gracious care and protection well knowing that you, who neither sleep nor slumber, are the watchful guardian of your favoured people. O watch over us, we pray, for good, that none of the evils which our sins have merited may befall us. Protect us both from the works and from the powers of darkness, and preserve us from all terrors and dangers through the night.

Let all our sins this day or at any former time committed, be removed out of your sight. Lift us into your presence that we may lie down with a sweet sense of your favour and a pleasurable assurance that you have accepted us in the Son of your love. For whom, and to whom, with your eternal self and the Holy Spirit, be all thanks and praise, and honour and glory, ascribed by us and by all your Church, from this time forth and for evermore. *Amen.*

6

O Lord our God, most high and mighty, most wise and holy, most just and good! You are, you were, and you will ever continue unspeakably blessed and glorious above all that we are able to express or conceive. You do not need the services of men or angels to make the least addition to your glory or bliss. In kindness and love you have been pleased to lay your commands upon us and to appoint that we should wait upon you in our present duties: which is the blissful employment of all the hosts of heaven.

You humble yourself when you see the things that are in heaven, or regard the worship of those blessed creatures above. O how wonderful then is your condescension that you should look down upon us, poor sinful creatures, who dwell in houses of clay and whose foundation is in the dust! Lord, what is man that you are mindful of him and the son of man that you care for him?

You cannot need us, or any thing of ours, O blessed God. We all stand in continual need of you, our only sovereign good, in need of your mercy and forgiveness, your grace and guidance, your blessing and assistance. Without these we can never hope to escape the misery which is the wages due to our sins, nor ever attain to that glory which is the free gift of God in Christ Jesus.

The desire of our souls, therefore, is to your name, O Lord, and to the remembrance of you. Our eyes are towards you and all our expectation is from you. We wait and call and depend upon you until you have mercy upon us according to our various needs, and according to the multitude of your tender mercies.

O remember not against us our former iniquities. Enter not into judgement with us according to our deserving; but according to your mercy remember us for your goodness' sake, O Lord. Blot out our transgressions as a cloud and justify us freely by your grace through the redemption that is in Christ Jesus. Bless us, O God of our salvation, in turning us from all our iniquities and in giving us grace, that we may repent and amend our lives according to your holy Word.

To this be pleased to enlighten our dark minds with the beams of your saving truth. O let us not be foolish but understand what the will of the Lord is. Reform our depraved wills, and incline them to a cheerful compliance with all the motions of your good Spirit. Regulate our unruly passions, purify our corrupt affections and convert all the faculties of our souls that they may be instruments of your glory, as they have been of your dishonour. Make our bodies fit temples for your Holy Spirit. Sanctify us wholly in body, soul and spirit, that we may adorn your gospel in all holy word and deed.

Cause us, O Lord, to hear your voice while we still can that we may make haste and not delay to keep your commandments. O keep us frequently and affectionately mindful of the shortness of our time, the frailty of our lives, and the uncertainty of our continuance in this impermanent world. Here we have no continuing city but are strangers and sojourners as all our fathers were.

O let the remembrance of this have a prevailing influence upon us to crucify the world to us and us to the world. Let it make us more deeply concerned for our everlasting welfare and more careful to make use of every present good for our soul's eternal advantage. Let the work of your grace be daily advancing in our hearts that we may grow in grace, as we grow in years, and be continually maturing for the full enjoyment of your glory.

The same things we ask also on behalf of all whom we ought to remember in our prayers. O forgive the sins, and relieve the miseries of your sinful creatures throughout the world. Enlarge the borders of your Church and add to it daily such as shall be saved. O that all who are called Christians may be Christians indeed, not only believing your Word but walking as becomes the gospel of Christ.

Let the Church which you have planted amongst us be your continual care. Watch over it, O Lord, for good. Preserve it night and day and let no weapon formed against it prosper. Give your judgements also, O God, unto the Queen that she may judge your people righteously and defeat their oppressors. Grant her always an interest in the hearts of her people and protection from the hands of her enemies. May she so rule and reign for you that she may come to live and reign for ever with you. Make all our magistrates to be God-fearing men who shun evil.

O that all who are called to serve you by Word and Sacrament may be in a special manner more blessed with compassionate hearts and exemplary lives. Make them wise to win souls, faithful, industrious and successful in their sacred office, as workmen that need not be ashamed. Bless and prosper all the seminaries of sound learning and religious education. Bless all orders and ranks of people amongst us. Let them all know you from the least to the greatest and so order their way of life aright that they may see the salvation of God.

Remember for good all those who have been in any way instrumental to our good. Let all who have injured us receive forgiveness at your hands. Look upon all that mourn in Zion. Give unto them a crown of beauty instead of ashes, the oil of joy instead of mourning, and the garment of praise instead of the spirit of despair. Teach those who are in health and prosperity to remember and provide for the time of trouble, sickness and death. Make all of every condition to be mindful of their duty that you may remember them in mercy and be their God and portion for ever.

Our own unworthiness would make us despair of

obtaining all these great and good things which we ask at your hands, O Lord. The remembrance of your tender mercy and your continual bounty puts life into our hopes and encouragement into our prayers and leaves us no reason to doubt of finding mercy with you. Blessed forever be your name that we have so much to confess of your goodness from our own experience, for by grace you have in so many things made us to differ from thousands of our fellow creatures.

O good Lord, continue your gracious favour to us and your fatherly care over us this night. As we go to rest after the labours of the day, so help us daily to do your work that we may enter into that rest which remains for your people at the close of life. Renew to us day by day your pardoning mercy and supply us daily with your grace. May we finish our course with joy and at the end of this life be received into your glory. All of this we ask in the name and for the sake of our only Redeemer for whom we thank you and to whom, with yourself, O Father, and the Holy Spirit our Comforter, in the unity of the ever blessed Trinity, be all praise and honour and glory ascribed by us and all the people of God, now and for evermore. *Amen.*

7

O Lord, great and glorious God, infinite in power, wisdom and goodness! You have created all things by your almighty hand! You sustain and order all things by your wise and righteous providence. Your mercy is everlasting and over all your works. Who is able to express, who is able to conceive, the exceeding riches of your grace and goodness? In what plentiful measure have your bounties been poured out upon us, your sinful creatures, who deserve nothing from you but to be forsaken and abhorred by you! This day and every day of our lives, O Lord, we have tasted of your mercy and been wholly preserved by your fatherly care.

Notwithstanding all your patience and gracious dealings

with us, and all the repeated pledges of your favour towards us, O how inadequately have we repaid your love! What improper responses have we made for all your great and continued goodness that we have experienced! Beside the guilt of our inbred corruption which, as a sore burden, hangs heavy upon us, we are amazed at the greatness and multitude of all our other sins that we have committed against you. We have sinned against the light and teachings of your gospel, against the dictates and strivings of your Spirit, against the love and sufferings of your Son and against all the patience and forbearance which you have exercised towards us.

O Lord, we have given you so great provocation that we have reason to fear lest you should forsake us utterly and cause the day of your patience to end. Well may we be afraid that you will grant us no more of that grace which we have so greatly abused, nor any supplies of that Holy Spirit whom we have so often resisted. What have we now to expect from you, O Lord? What but judgement if it were not that your mercy triumphs over judgement!

Your Word assures us that you delight not in the death of sinners, but rather that they should turn to you and live. Therefore you still leave us these opportunities to plead with you for the life of our souls. But what have we to plead? Nothing, O Lord, in ourselves. Our hope is only in you. We plead, therefore, your own gracious nature, your merciful inclinations and your exceeding great and precious promises which you have freely made to repenting sinners.

You have sent your only Son to be our almighty Saviour and he that did no sin was manifested to take away our sins. O then for his sake be pleased to pity us, to spare us and to forgive us. Turn away your wrath from us. Receive us into your blessed favour and comfort us with the sure persuasion that our transgressions are forgiven.

Such is the infirmity of our nature that without your grace we have not the least power to keep ourselves even from the smallest sins: O grant us the increase of your grace and the help of your good Spirit that we may be fortified against all temptation and be made your willing and faithful servants. Be pleased, O Lord, to continue to disclose and manifest yourself to our souls, that we may truly know you, the only true God, and Jesus Christ whom you have sent.

Give us power from on high that we may be able to live according to that light which you are pleased to impart to us, that we may not hold the truth in unrighteousness but may walk in the light as children of the light. O let us not be almost but altogether and truly Christians. Let us be true penitents, sincere converts and sound believers. You who work all in all, finish in us the work of your grace that we may have cause to give you praise and glory to all eternity.

These things, Lord, we ask, not only for ourselves, but for all who partake of our nature, for all whom you have made capable of eternal happiness. More especially we pray for your whole Church, wherever and in whatever circumstances it exists on the earth. We pray for the Queen's majesty, and all our rulers and judges, for our ministers and teachers, for our relations and neighbours, our friends and benefactors and for your afflicted ones whatsoever be their trials and troubles. O supply all their wants and fulfil all their desires in such a manner as your wisdom sees best, for your own mercy's sake in Christ Jesus.

You, Lord, are the great preserver of men, who have kept and blessed us this day and all our days. Praised be your name for all your goodness which we have so long and largely experienced. O make us aware of your kindness and thankful for it as we truly ought to be. Take care of us, O Lord, and be gracious to us this night. Give us not only bodily rest in our beds but rest for our souls in your blessed self. Be our God and guide, our hope and help, our joy and comfort, our All in All, this night and for evermore. *Amen*

(iv) The Lord's Prayer extended

O God the Father of our Lord Jesus Christ by eternal generation; the Father of all things by temporal creation and the Father of your people by adoption and spiritual generation — what manner of love is this, that we who have been rebels against heaven, slaves of Satan, and the children deserving only your wrath, should be made children of the Most High and heirs of everlasting glory! We are yours, O Lord, for you have made us out of nothing; you have created us anew after we had condemned ourselves through sin, and you have looked upon us in our spiritual death and summoned us to live. You are in heaven! O that we may ascend there in heart and mind, and with all humility worship at the feet of your glorious Majesty! You are our Father! O that we may confidently and delightfully draw near to you as dear children! May we also love one another as brothers and be united as children of the same heavenly Father.

O that all the world may give you the glory due to your name so that you may be better known, feared, loved and honoured both by us and by all men as our supreme Lord and as our chief good. O that we may glorify you as we ought in our thoughts and our desires and in our words and ways!

O that the kingdom of sin and Satan may be increasingly weakened till they are utterly destroyed, that the powers on earth may use reverently the authority which you have given them, that all the kingdoms of the world may become the kingdoms of our Lord and of his Christ, and Jerusalem be made the joy and praise of the whole earth! O that Christ may dwell and rule in our hearts by his Spirit and grace, and make us a willing people and faithful subjects of his holy kingdom. May he still reign over us here till we are fitted to reign with him in glory for evermore! O blessed and only Ruler, let your kingdom come so powerfully into us that we may always do your will faithfully and unreservedly.

May your will and Word, O Lord, and the way of salvation be known everywhere on earth. Let the light of your gospel shine and prevail and win more converts daily throughout the world. O send the means of grace where they are absent and make them prosperous and successful where they are now. Let not the will of our sinful nature nor the ways of the world govern us, but let the Word and the will of our God be the rule of our lives to guide and direct us in all our conduct. Make us conform more to all your will requires of us and more submissive to all it lays upon us. Yes, make us pleased with whatever is your will so that, loving your Word and delighting to do your will, we may joyfully and cheerfully serve you as your glorious angels and saints above, for whom it is heaven to please and enjoy the Lord.

Until we are fit for the life to come, give us, O Father (of your gracious bounty), all that is necessary and conducive to our well-being. Preserve us from all the snares and dangers of both prosperity and affliction. When we have this world's goods, O that we may use them wisely and devoutly to your glory. When you take them from us make us contented, patient and thankful and more concerned with that true good which shall not be taken away. O all-wise and merciful God, we beg that we may always be in that physical state which you know to be best for our souls and grant that all which we possess in this life may help to prepare us for the life to come.

We are ashamed and grieved that we have so much and so long dishonoured your blessed name, disobeyed your holy Word and abused your rich mercy. We desire to be reconciled to our God, to be humbled and to be penitent for our sins, and to ask your gracious favour in Christ Jesus for pardoning them. Forgive us, we beseech you, O Father of mercies, for his sake all the sins we have ever committed against you. We especially beg to be forgiven for those ruinous and presumptuous sins which we have at any time committed against the promptings of the Holy Spirit and the voice of our own consciences, and which have filled our souls with the dread of your wrath. O give us indications which would persuade and assure our hearts that you will be merciful to us. Incline our hearts, O Lord, to forgive others as we need to be forgiven and to be merciful as we desire to obtain mercy.

O God of all grace, by the power of your Holy Spirit subdue our sins that they may not prevail against us or injure us for the future. Do not allow us ever to be tempted more than we are able to bear with the strength which your grace supplies. Enable us to avoid all the temptations we can, and be strong in the Lord so as to overcome those we must encounter. We are poor, frail creatures but you are the Lord Almighty. O do protect us, we beseech you, by your powerful help and so keep us from falling that we may never be made a prey to the cruel murderer of souls, nor be delivered into those bitter pains of eternal death which are the sad wages of our sin. Grant that we may find a way to escape every snare and be preserved for your heavenly kingdom.

Yours is the kingdom, O Lord most high! You are the King of all the world and happy are those who are guided by your good Spirit as the willing subjects of your spiritual kingdom. We desire and beg that we may all be found in that number. Save, Lord, and let the King of heaven hear us when we call.

We ask great things of you but not too great for the Almighty God to grant, for yours is the power and you are able to do for us exceedingly abundantly, even above all that we can ask or think. O reveal your glorious power to do things worthy of God which only your blessed self can do — in forgiving, healing and helping us who are helpless and hopeless in ourselves.

Yours is the glory, O God and by the wonders of your grace you glorify yourself by bringing to salvation those that were lost.

Therefore, though we are exceedingly guilty and utterly unworthy, yet we pray and hope that you will glorify your mercy by remembering us in our sinful condition and bringing to us what we lack and need. We would forsake every other refuge to come to you, for our expectation is from you and we are wholly dependent upon you alone. We trust in your gracious goodness through the merits and mediation of our blessed Redeemer, looking for the mercy of our Lord Jesus Christ unto eternal life.

O great and glorious Lord God, whose kingdom rules over all, to you who do whatever you please in heaven and on earth, to you who are pleased to show forth all your glory to the blessed saints and angels in your presence, to you be glory in the highest, and all thanks and praise be ascribed, by us and by all the world, for ever and ever. *Amen.*

3

PRAYERS FOR USE ON
THE LORD'S DAY

(i) Introduction

The Lord's Day was taken very seriously not only as a day of rest but also as a day for worship, special devotions, and extra reflection upon the Word, both preached and read. Here are prayers for use by the family together in the morning and evening and by individual members at midday and as each one prepares for worship, for hearing the Word and for receiving the Sacrament.

Usually Holy Communion was once a month and so the major services on most Sundays in an Anglican setting were those of Morning and Evening Prayer, along perhaps with the first half of the Order for Holy Communion (the Ministry of the Word only). These services are very much services of the Word and thus to pray for a right hearing and reception of that Word was most appropriate. Further, the fact that Holy Communion was not taken every week meant that, because of its infrequency, there was the possibility of serious preparation for its monthly reception — hence the petitionary and meditative prayers both before and after receiving the sacramental body and blood of Christ.

The Lord's Day is also a day for petition and intercession for God's Church, for its growth in numbers and holiness and for the faithfulness of its ministry. Hence there are three prayers addressed to God on behalf of the Church militant in Britain and in the whole world.

(ii) Two Morning prayers

1

O most blessed and gracious Lord God, your almighty hand has brought us out of nothing to enjoy the comforts of life, and your free grace has called us out of a state worse than nothing to the hope of your heavenly glory! We bless your name because you have conducted us safely through all states and conditions of our lives to see the comforting light of this day. We glorify you that we have another day of grace in which to seek the things belonging to our eternal peace.

We adore you for having so far considered the good of our souls as to set apart this day for holy purposes, that we might engage in a solemn attendance upon you in whose service consists all our honour and happiness. O God, how much higher might we have been in your favour, how much nearer to you, and fitter for your heavenly kingdom had we rightly used for our spiritual benefit those means of grace which you have been pleased to make available for us!

But we have been cruel to our own souls, as well as disobedient to you, our Lord. Many times we have lost the opportunities of appearing before you. We have shunned as a task what was our highest privilege and, even when we have set ourselves to seek your face, it has been with such coldness and dulness, such wanderings and distractions, that you might justly abhor our souls, and despise our services.

Be pleased to look upon us in the Son of your love, who is the Lord our peace and our righteousness. Forgive us all that is past, in which we have neglected your work or performed it amiss or done what was inconsistent with it. Help us, O God of our salvation, and deliver us both from the bands and burden of our guilt. Purge away all our sins, for the glory of your name. O let them not stand as a partition-wall to hinder the ascent of our prayers to you or the descent of your blessings upon us. Let your peace and love shine into our souls that we may see the genuine happiness of your chosen and draw water with joy out of the wells of salvation.

O let us not rest in any outward forms of godliness which deny true spiritual power. Let us not profess Christianity unless we are moved with its life and power. Let the Gospel of our Lord, and the graces of your good Spirit, shine forth in our lives to your glory, our heavenly Father.

O gracious God be with us and with all the ministers and stewards of your mysteries who are this day to speak in your name. Furnish them with abilities necessary for their great work. Enable them to suit themselves to the capacities and necessities of their different hearers.

Grant, Lord, unto us and unto all the hearers of your holy Word, humble and teachable spirits that we may receive your truth lovingly so as to profit and grow by it. Remove all the hindrances of our spiritual improvement that your Word may have free course, and be glorified amongst us. Let us this day go forth in the strength of the Lord our God and prosper and increase by divine help. Let your grace and blessing accompany all our endeavours; and, having served you imperfectly upon earth, may we attain to the full enjoyment of you in heaven and glorify you in the perfection of holiness for ever and ever.

Let your grace and blessing, your love and fellowship, your direction and assistance, O heavenly Father, Son and Holy Spirit be with us and with all for whom we ought to pray, this day and for evermore. *Amen.*

2

O Lord, the great almighty God, you are the giver of life and strength and of all grace and goodness. Without you we can do nothing but through your gracious assistance we are enabled to do all things which you require of us.

We humbly ask you to be graciously present with us and powerfully assist us in all the duties of your holy service. O forgive our transgressions that separate you from our souls. Remember not the sins against us which may justly provoke you to hide your face from us; but according to your mercy remember us, O Lord, and accept us and our poor imperfect services at the hands and for the sake of Jesus Christ.

O leave us not to the dulness and hardness, the vanity and deceitfulness, of our own depraved hearts. Show the power of your heavenly grace to fix our thoughts, to kindle our affections and to keep us in a devout and holy frame of mind. Work mightily in us, we beseech you, and give us that preparation of heart, without which we cannot serve you acceptably or enjoy communion with you.

O let us not come before you in formality and hypocrisy but let our souls, and all that is within us, be taken up in a reverent, faithful, and affectionate attendance upon you. Nor let us serve you out of constraint, only because we must, but with all readiness and gladness, delighting to be so engaged. Let your pleasure be ours and your service be the joy of our hearts.

O help us so to sanctify your day that your day may be a means of promoting the sanctification of our souls. Let us engage in spiritual exercises befitting this holy day and not profane it by vain purposes. On the Lord's Day may we abound in the work of the Lord − not according to our own works or by finding our own pleasure or by speaking our own words in the day which you have hallowed for yourself. May we rest from all our sinful ways as well as from our common labours. May we so delight ourselves in the Lord that you may give us the desire of our hearts.

Bless to us your Word, O gracious Father, and all the means of grace which through your favour we enjoy. Let us never use them in vain or to our hurt. May they ever serve to instruct our minds, reform our lives and save our souls. May we expect to find good from your ordinances. Let us never be disappointed of our hope in the means of grace but let us be edified by them. Let us grow in grace and in the knowledge of our Lord Jesus Christ till the purpose of

them be fully realised within us and we are made such as
you require us to be in all holy conversation and godliness.

You have said that they who love your law have great
peace and that they shall never be turned from your way.
O dear Lord increase our love for your Word, which even
the angels desire to look into. Make our souls pliable and
submissive that we may be ruled by it in all things and be
cast in the very mould of your gospel.

O heavenly Father, command a blessing upon all our
godly designs and endeavours this day. Bless your servants
whom you have appointed to break the bread of life to our
souls that they may speak your Word as they ought to speak
it and give to every one his portion in due season. Let the
word which they deliver be for the conviction and comfort
of many souls.

You, who have the key of David which opens and never
shuts; you, who speak to the heart and give the increase,
open our understanding to receive your truth both in the
light and love of it. Set it home powerfully upon our hearts
and root it so deeply in our souls that the fruits of it may
appear in our lives. May we not be forgetful hearers but
faithful doers of your Word.

Grant, O gracious God, that our services this day may
be such as may tend to our advantage in the great day of
your appearing and glory. Let us hallow these sabbaths upon
earth that hereafter we may be admitted to the joyful
celebration of the eternal sabbath in heaven. There, with
the Church triumphant, may we laud and magnify your
glorious name and enjoy your love and sing your praise for
ever.

Now Lord, for the addition of this sabbath we bless you.
For the benefit of your Word and for the ordinances of your
worship we glorify your name. For all the means of grace
and the hope of glory, to you, the God of all grace, be praise
and honour and glory rendered by us and by all your people,
from this time forth and for evermore. *Amen.*

(iii) A Midday prayer

O Lord the God of glory, you fill heaven and earth with your presence, fill my heart I pray with your grace and with a consciousness that your eye is ever watching me. May I conduct myself as in your immediate presence and serve you on earth as you are served above, where thousand upon thousand minister unto you and ten thousand times ten thousand stand before you. Happy are they who surround your throne and are ever occupied in the contemplation of your Majesty and the fruition of your love. They have an everlasting end put to all their sins and troubles and temptations. They have their souls perfected in holiness, their hearts filled with joy, and their mouths opened to utter without ceasing the everlasting praises of their God.

O Lord, look down from heaven, upon the habitation of your holiness and your glory, and behold with pity the poor remnant of your heritage who are still engaged in their warfare and pilgrimage in this present evil world. They are surrounded with many and powerful enemies and are groaning for deliverance from the bondage of corruption in order that they may be brought into the glorious liberty of the children of God.

O good Lord, pardon every one of us who now prepare and set ourselves to seek your face and to meet and enjoy you in the ordinances of worship. Though we are not cleansed according to the purification of the sanctuary, accept us in your beloved Son according to what we have; and fill us with your good Spirit to make us what we should be. O give unto me, in particular, though the most unworthy of your creatures, a devout and contrite heart, that I may not merely utter words of prayer, or rest in any forms of godliness, but may serve you with my spirit, and lift up my heart to the Lord and as much as is possible have my life centred in heaven.

It is good for men to draw near to God in whose service consists all our honour and bliss. O let my heart rejoice in seeking the Lord. Let me with great liveliness, love and cheerfulness frequent your ways, study your Word, admire your works and magnify your name.

I bless you, my God that you have given me an understanding to know you, a heart to love you and a soul capable of waiting upon you in the duties of your holy service and of enjoying you in your heavenly glory. I bless you for all the opportunities and advantages which I have to serve you and to work out my salvation. I adore you for the ministry of reconciliation committed to your servants, for all their labours, and writings and preaching, and for all other means of grace and assistance in this my warfare.

O give me such a love for your Word that I may value it above all the wealth of the world. May I relish it better than all the pleasures of the flesh and esteem it more than my necessary food. Enable me to receive not only its light but also its love so that I may live and grow by it and attain the salvation which it sets before me. Give me, Lord, a heart always to fear you and to keep your commandments that all may go well with me, both now and forever.

Let me so make your Word the rule of my life that it may also be the ground of my hope. While it is sounding in my ears apply it with an irresistible energy to my soul that I may be obedient to it in the day of your power. Let there be such a transcript of the gospel in my life that I may not only hear what it says but be such as it describes.

O gracious God, continue the light and joyful sound of your gospel amongst us. Help us so to use it rightly and to profit by it, that we may have reason to bless and praise you for it to all eternity. O that every Lord's Day may add yet more and more to our stature in Christ Jesus. May we so sanctify your sabbaths now that in the end we may enjoy the sabbath of your eternal rest, there to dwell in your sight and rejoice in love and triumph in your praise for evermore. *Amen*.

(iv) Two Evening prayers

1

O Lord our God, you are infinitely good, and you have shown us what is good and what you require of us that it may go well with us both now and to all eternity. You send out your light and your truth amongst us. You make the way of life and salvation plain before us. You give us many opportunities to take us further in the knowledge of that way which leads to the kingdom of your glory. We have line upon line, and precept upon precept. You send your messengers early and late to open and apply your Word, to give us calls and warnings, directions and exhortations, and to promote by all possible means our edification here and our salvation for ever.

You have not been absent from us, O Lord, but we have been exceedingly unavailable to ourselves. O how we have loved darkness rather than light and chosen to follow our own foolish and hurtful lusts rather than to be guided by your blessed Word! So little have we made use of that which you have put into our hands, that you may justly take away the gospel of the kingdom from us and give it to another people who shall bring forth fruits more worthy of it. Because you have called and we have refused to hear, and you have stretched forth your hands and we have not taken any notice, you may leave us to our own perverseness and impenitence to add sin to sin till our transgressions become our ruin.

O Lord God, merciful and gracious, we humbly beg you not to enter into judgement with your servants but in mercy pardon all our contempt of your Word and our abuse of all the means of grace which you have afforded us. Help us for the time to come to make right use of such gracious opportunities to the glory of your name and the benefit of our own souls.

As the rain descends from heaven and does not return

there, but waters the earth and makes it fruitful, so let your Word not return unto you void but let it accomplish your good pleasure and prosper in that for which you are pleased to send it. O make it instrumental and effective to bring your grace where it is not, and to establish and increase it where it is. Let it build us all up in the fear and love of God and in the knowledge and faith of our Lord Jesus Christ.

Though we cannot claim upon reviewing this day that we have duly kept a day holy to the Lord, yet let it not be a lost day to us nor let your Word be as water spilt upon the ground. Let your good Spirit bring your Word to our remembrance and cause it to be an engrafted Word, able and effective to save our souls. As we have been taught how we ought to walk and to please our God, so help us to walk more worthy of you and be more ready to perform every good work which may be pleasing in your sight through Jesus Christ.

At his hands, O merciful God, we ask your gracious acceptance of our praise and thanksgiving for all the blessings which you have so freely conferred upon us and so long continued to us. You have dealt graciously with us, O blessed Lord, and been exceedingly kind to us, not only beyond all that we had reason to expect, but above all that we are able to express.

We bless your name, O heavenly Father, that in so many respects you have made us to differ from multitudes in the world who are destitute both of the comforts of this life, and the hope of a better which, through your special favour, we enjoy. We acknowledge your hand in everything and we desire to ascribe to you all the praise and glory. Particularly would our souls now bless you for the mercies which we have experienced this day, for your house open to us, for the Word of salvation sounding in our ears and for your blessed Spirit striving in our hearts.

O that we may not receive the grace of God in vain and that your mercies may not be wasted upon us! Let us act more worthy of that care and kindness which we have so long and largely experienced. Let us thankfully receive and carefully make good use of your distinguishing favours. Let us not provoke you to withdraw your tender mercies from us but rather may you continue to show your accustomed goodness to us, to increase and multiply your blessings upon us and to rejoice over us.

In mercy pardon all that which your pure and holy eyes have seen amiss this day in any of our thoughts and desires, our words or actions. O pardon our neglect of what we should have done and the guilt which we have contracted in all that we have attempted to do. Forgive the transgressions of our misuse of holy things and enter not into judgement with us even according to the best of our works and services; but overlook all our sins and failings and imperfections for the sake of our great Mediator and Redeemer, who appears in your presence and is at your right hand to make intercession for us. To him, as the blessed Author of our hopes and happiness, and to you, our Father, who condescended to deliver him up for us, and to that blessed Spirit who has revealed him to us, be all praise and honour and glory, humbly and heartily ascribed by us and by all your Church, now and for evermore. *Amen.*

2

O Lord, you are good to the soul that seeks you. By numberless invitations and by all the endearments of your love, you encourage poor sinners to come to you. You do not bid us seek your face in vain, or serve for nothing. You have pleasure in the prosperity of your servants and give not according to our poor and imperfect services but according to your infinitely rich and tender mercies. You give us eternal life through Jesus Christ our Lord.

It is not anything in your laws, O gracious Lord, but the sinfulness of our sinful nature that makes any of them seem grievous to us. They are all holy and just and good, tending only to promote our present and eternal happiness. Nor is it anything in your blessed service but the disposition of our own deceitful hearts that makes any part of that employment tedious to us, which is the work and joy of angels and which it is our wisdom, our honour, our interest and our happiness to perform.

Holy God, before you we are all unclean and all our righteousness is as filthy rags. We can never hope to be justified in your sight upon the account of any works or worth of our own. By our own hearts and deeds we are reproved and condemned and should be left speechless in the judgement, if you, O Lord, should call us to account according to the merits even of our best services.

We desire to take refuge under the shadow of our crucified Saviour and to be found in him, not having our own righteousness, but that which is by the faith of Jesus Christ. In this faith alone is the shame of our nakedness covered and all our sinful deformities hidden from your eyes. We beg you to forgive us mercifully and receive us graciously and love us freely in the Son of your love in whom you are well pleased.

Command a blessing, we pray you, O Lord, upon the Word which this day we have heard and upon all the means of grace that have been used for the good of our souls. It is not he who plants, nor he who waters, but you, our God, who give the increase. Be pleased to accompany the preaching of your Word with the powerful influences of your grace and Holy Spirit, that it may be the delight of life to our souls and the power of God to our salvation.

O let us so hide your Word in our hearts that we may not (as we have done) sin against you but may have it as a treasure within us to help us in every hour of temptation and in every time of need. Apply it to our hearts that we may walk more humbly and closely with our God and more conscientiously and circumspectly before you. May we be so obedient to the holy precepts of your Word that finally we may enjoy the great and precious promises contained in it.

Continue to us, O gracious Lord, the light of your gospel and all the happy opportunities which we enjoy for our souls' advantage. Preserve us also by your grace from the curse of barrenness. May your ordinances not rise up in judgement against us but make them effective for our good. Cause them to accomplish in us all the purposes of your grace and let their sanctifying power shine forth with a convincing splendour in our lives.

Now we give thanks to you, O Lord God, our heavenly Father, for the mercies of this day and for your great mercy and goodness that has followed us all the days of our lives. O how wonderful is your patience and long-suffering that you should all day stretch forth your hands to a rebellious and contradictory people! How unwearied your kindness and love that you still load us with benefits, despite our past abuse of them, and impart even the greatest mercies to us who have deserved nothing but judgements at your hands.

Blessed be your name, O most merciful Father, that you have defended us from so many dangers in our lives which threatened to destroy us. You delivered us out of so many troubles under which we should have sunk and perished if you had not been near to us and done great things for us. We bless you for our health and plenty, peace and liberty, for the use of our reason, limbs and senses. We thank you for our comforts, the kindness of friends, safety from our enemies, the benefits and refreshments of society and the success and prosperity of our affairs in the world.

Above all we bless you for the mercies and blessings relating to the world to come, for Jesus Christ and all spiritual blessings in heavenly places in him. We bless you for remembering us in our poverty and for sending eternal redemption to us by the hands of your dear Son. We bless you for the light and direction of your Word, for the teachings and strivings, the assistance and consolation of your Spirit and for all the means by which you do us good. We bless you for all your grace wrought in us and bestowed upon us and for all the discoveries and hopes of eternal glory which you have given to us.

O how infinitely indebted we are to the kindness and love of God our Saviour! O that we may ever be aware of this and thankful as we ought! With all that you have given us, blessed Lord, give us also hearts filled with your love and lifted up in your praise and devoted to your service.

We can only acknowledge the debt which we can never pay. We cannot praise you according to the riches of your grace and the multitude of your mercies, but we desire to bless and praise you with all the capacities and abilities with which you have blessed us. Help us, O Lord, our God, to glorify your name not only in uttering your praise, but in so entirely devoting ourselves to your service that we may be yours in faithfulness, and in the sincerity of our hearts, even all the days of our lives.

O make us truly penitent and humbled for all which this day we have done amiss. Make us sincerely thankful for all the good that we have received and for all which you have, in any manner or measure, enabled us to do aright. The evil is from ourselves alone, and to us belongs shame and confusion of face for it; but all the good is of your free grace and mercy. To your blessed name, O Lord, our God, be all the praise and glory rendered with the most appreciative and grateful hearts, now and for evermore. *Amen.*

(v) Two prayers for before and after hearing the Word

1. Before

O most blessed Lord, the God of all grace! You are pleased to send out your light and your truth among us both to disclose our sins and also to make the way of life and salvation plain to us. Be pleased also to send the Spirit of your Son into our hearts, to make your truth plain to our understanding and the sweetness of life to our souls. O Lord, open our ears and draw our attention to the instructions that shall be given to us, that we may receive your Word with all carefulness and meekness, with all readiness and gladness, with a sincere delight in it and a hearty desire to live and grow by it. Strengthen our memories that we may treasure and retain what we hear, that we may not let it slip but derive substantial benefit from it both now and to all eternity.

O gracious God, teach us to profit and to improve in accordance with the means of grace which we enjoy through your mercy. Let the Word which shall sound in our ears, sink down also into our hearts, take root within us and produce in our lives the fruits of righteousness. Let us not be forgetful hearers but faithful doers of your Word. O let the immortal seed of this heavenly Word produce such principles of grace and holiness in our hearts that they may be in us as a well of water springing up to everlasting life. Make us so obedient to your holy precepts that we may also inherit the glorious promises of your Word.

O instruct our teachers and direct the stewards of your mysteries to give to each his portion at the appropriate time. While your servants are planting and watering, O God, bestow your blessing and give them an abundant harvest. Make the waters of your sanctuary heal our souls. Make your Word as fire in the mouths of your messengers that it may burn into our souls and reveal your Spirit and your power. Let it be mighty through God to demolish defences and subdue all opposition to obedience to Christ. Come down among us, O God of our salvation, and cause your Word to accomplish your great and glorious work upon our hearts that we may have reason to praise and glorify you to all eternity. *Amen.*

2. After

We bless you, O Lord, the living God, for you maintain our physical life and provide for us that heavenly food by which we are to live forever. It has now been delivered and received; but, the blessing is in your hands, O gracious God, to make it prosperous and successful in gaining and saving immortal souls. Be pleased to plant your Word in the heart and make it abide there until it has done your will and fully accomplished your work. Make use of it now to build us up in the faith of Christ and to progress in all holiness of life. Let every hearer become a doer of your word that we may all, in this world, be blessed in our deeds and, hereafter, be for ever blessed in the joy of our Lord.

O that all who have been convinced of their sins may also be converted to you that they may not only think of the holy change that has been worked in them but seek incessantly to attain it. Let your blessed Spirit so prevail with them that his influences may not be lost until they have perfected the work of grace within them.

O make your Word mighty through God that it may plant your grace where it is absent, increase it where it exists, and bring us all nearer to you and in complete conformity to your image. Let us find our knowledge clearer and more spiritual, our faith firmer and more active, and all our graces continually increasing in strength and activity in our souls. Let us so hear your Word that our souls may live before you both now and forever. *Amen.*

(vi) Four prayers for before and after the Lord's Supper

1. Before

O what am I, poor unworthy sinful wretch, that I should go to the Lord's table and participate in what is provided for his saints! Great God: my guilt, my shame, and my fear incline me to withdraw and to conclude that it would be presumptuous and vain for me ever to expect such high honour and favour from your hands. I could not presume to approach so near to your divine Majesty except that you are pleased to invite and command us to come to you. Nor could I ever hope for such heavenly blessings at your hands, O Lord, were it not that you are infinitely good and kind, even to those who deserve nothing but to be forsaken and abhorred by you. Instead of stretching forth a hand of mercy to invite me to your table, you might with the rod of your wrath, dash me in pieces as a potter's vessel. Instead of entertaining me with the bread of life and the cup of blessing, you might give me the bread and water of affliction and cast me into the lowest pit where I should cry in vain for one drop of water to cool my tongue.

Lord, seeing that you are pleased to command that those who have failed should come to you for help, you have appointed this sacrament as a means of extending to them pardon and grace. Since I need so desperately your pardoning mercy and your sanctifying grace, I come, Lord, polluted and unfit, to appear before you. I dare not but come, knowing that I shall be lost if I keep away from you. I come not, Lord, because I am worthy, but because you are rich in mercy. I come as the hungry to be fed, and as the sick and maimed to recover and be healed. I come that I may wash in the blood of your dear Son and be cleansed; that I may receive out of his infinite fulness all that is lacking in my wretched self, and that I may so touch my Saviour as to derive virtue from him to heal my infirmities and equip myself for his service.

O that I may come in the most humble manner, with all reverence and godly fear, and with the most earnest longings after Christ Jesus. May I also come with the heartiest resolutions to live for him who, of his infinite mercy, was pleased to die for me! Instruct me, O Lord, and assist me in the examination and preparation of myself in order that I may come with a clean and peaceful conscience to partake of this holy ordinance. Before I draw near to your altar purify my heart by repentance and by faith in the blood of our adorable Redeemer. O let me receive a crucified Saviour into a broken and contrite heart. Make me so willing and obedient that I may derive good from the ordinance and enjoy in it, not only a representation, but a rich participation also, of his dying love.

O enter, my Lord, and do not be a stranger to the soul which has been purchased by your blood. Enrich your ordinance with your presence that I may find him whom my soul desires to love and whose love is better than wine.

Blessed Jesus, make yourself known to my soul in this breaking of bread and let me receive such life from you as will enable me to live unto you. Make me to know that you abide in me by the Spirit which you have graciously given to me.

Blessed Saviour, weigh not my merits but your own for I have deserved nothing at your hands but wrath. I could not presume to ask you for anything if you had not redeemed me with your precious blood. I can never be worthy of you but you can give me such views, dispositions, and affections, that I may eat and drink worthily of the feast to which I am invited. Come to my help, O blessed Emmanuel, that I may participate of your sacred body crucified and your precious blood shed for us with such discernment, reverence, penitence, faith, love, and thankfulness as I ought to do. May I receive these symbols of your love for my present consolation and my everlasting salvation.

You who have prepared a table in this wilderness with heavenly provisions for our souls, prepare my soul, dear Lord, for these provisions. Give me spiritual appetite as well as spiritual sustenance that, as the hart pants after the stream of water, so may my soul pant after you, O God. Let me feel an intense desire to eat this passover. Make me so to open my mouth that you may fill my hungry soul with good things and so to lift up the everlasting doors of my heart that the King of Glory may come in. Come, Lord, and dwell in my heart by faith and abide with my spirit to my dying hour.

O make your sacrament healing and a delight to my soul. Make it also a sacrament which seals the pardon of my sins and gives me assurance of your love. As you seal the covenant of grace, O let me seal the covenant of obedience. May I come in such a devout and acceptable manner to your table that I may return from it with my conscience quietened, my corruptions subdued, my graces increased, my soul encouraged, and with my heart enlarged to live in obedience to your commands.

O Lord, to whom should I resort but to you, my life, my strength, and my Redeemer! You, who call unto yourself

the labouring and heavy-laden sinners, help me so to come
to you that in you I may find rest for my soul. You, who
have commanded us to share our bread with the hungry,
O break the bread of life to all of us who hunger and thirst
after righteousness, and give us, O Lord God our heavenly
Father, this bread for ever. Since you are pleased to continue
to give us the liberty and advantage of this sacrament to
nourish and revive our souls, create in our hearts a higher
esteem and a greater love for it. In our preparation before
we eat and drink at your table, in our communicating there,
and our conversation after, O teach and help us to act in
a way that is fitting for the redeemed of the Lord and the
living members of Jesus Christ.

Hear me, O Lord my God, and forgive me. Bless and
direct me, stimulate and assist me in the work before me.
Deal graciously with me that I may perform all my duties
heartily as to the Lord and acceptable in your sight, through
Jesus Christ, your beloved Son, my only Mediator and
Advocate. *Amen and Amen.*

2. Before

Blessed be my God who again is pleased to call me to the
reconciliation feast. Despite all my breaches with him and
all my offences against him, he grants me a forgiveness again
and seals my pardon afresh in the precious blood of his dear
Son, which was shed to take away the sins of the world.

At your gracious invitation, Lord, I am bold to come,
looking for that blessed benefit which I know myself so
unworthy to receive that you may justly shut the doors of
mercy against me, and withhold your saving good from me.
But your mercies, blessed God, are not for the deserving
and worthy but for the miserable and needy. O let me find
them, needy and miserable as I am, according to the riches
of your bounty and according to the greatness of my need.

I have no power for this great work but I will go in your
strength, O Lord, my God. Give me, I beseech you, the

motives of which you approve and achieve in me what you require. O let me find your hand upon me, your help with me and your grace sufficient for me.

O that I may see your power and your glory as I have seen you in the sanctuary! That I may share in the heavenly entertainment provided for your children and eat and drink in your presence that bread of life and that cup of blessing which shall be the life of my soul and make my heart glad with the joy of my salvation.

O what shall I do at your house and your table, O Lord, if you are not present to receive and entertain me? O that you would, in wonderful condescension, leave the heavens and come down and make me experience your presence with me, and the power of your Spirit upon me, and that loving-kindness of yours which is better than life itself.

O let not the great Lord and lover of souls be as a stranger to my soul, but let him look down and disclose himself and remember me in saving mercy, where he feeds his flock and provides it with rest. Let me now taste and see, to the satisfaction of my soul, how good the Lord is.

I desire to take shelter under the shadow of my Redeemer's wings and to be found in Christ Jesus, clothed with his righteousness which is sufficient to atone for all my guilt, and also to satisfy all my needs, and make me complete in the sight of God and fit for the happiness of his chosen. O God of all grace, give me, I beseech you, a share in that great redemption which your beloved Son has purchased for a ruined world that my soul may magnify the Lord and my spirit may rejoice in God my Saviour.

You, who are able to bring me into the bonds of the new covenant, let me enter into it voluntarily and cheerfully, not as one who is averse to the terms that it proposes, but as one who longs to enjoy the blessings which it offers.

O make me ready for your power and may I this day experience, O Lord, the powerful workings of your blessed Spirit to open and enlarge my heart, and make me ready and fit to receive him who stands and knocks into my soul, even Christ Jesus the Lord.

O how unworthy I am, Lord, that you should come under my roof; how unworthy to eat the crumbs that fall from your table! But your infinite merits can cover all my sins and unworthiness and present me to the just and holy Majesty of heaven as if I had not sinned. O deal graciously with me, my Lord and my God, I beseech you, and forgive, heal and help me. Exercise your power and pity towards me and come into my soul with all the blessings and consolations which you have taught us to expect from your hands.

O Lord, my soul is polluted and unclean, but your precious blood can cleanse me from all my sins and defilements and make me a fit dwelling place for your Holy Spirit. O speak the Word and I shall be clean and whole, and my soul shall live and for ever bless your name.

Assist me mercifully, O Lord, in my designs and efforts to obtain the blessed fruits of which you have made me capable. O forgive my unworthiness, cover my sins, help my infirmities, dispel my dulness, and prepare me to meet you. Draw me to yourself that I may enjoy you; and let me possess you *now*, as far as my poor capacity will allow, and *afterwards*, in all your fulness, for ever and ever.

O may your sacrament now be the means to establish me. Let it impart into my soul grace sufficient for me out of the fulness of Christ Jesus. Let it be the means of rendering me lively and constant in the performance of every duty. What I lack in myself, Lord, supply, and make me what I ought to be for your mercy's sake. *Amen. Amen.*

3. After

Glory be to you, O Lord our God, who in our extreme need of a redeemer, made such gracious provision for our souls by sending your Son to die for our sins and to save us when we were lost. Blessed be your name, for he who offered himself upon the cross for us is pleased to offer himself to us at his table. There I have been tasting the fruits of his love and receiving my share among the redeemed of the Lord. O blessed be God for so great a mercy!

I bless you, my God, for your mercy in sending us a Saviour. Without him all other mercies would be of no avail and would do me no good. I bless you that you did not withhold your Son, your only Son from us, but made him atone for our sins and become the life and food of our souls.

I sat down in his presence and it was a delight to me. I have been entertained at the table of the Lord who spread his love over me. It was love that gave me the Saviour whom I have been receiving and the opportunity to rest and feast my soul upon him.

Return to your rest, O my soul, for the Lord has dealt bountifully with you. You received life at the hands of him who forgives all your sins and heals your diseases. He not only saves you from destruction but crowns you with loving-kindness and tender mercies. He fills your mouth with tender utterances, with pardon and peace, with the riches of his grace and the pledges of his glory.

Blessed be my God for the Bread which came down from heaven to give life to the world. Blessed be your name, O gracious Lord, for my share in this highest expression of your wonderful love and bounty.

Eternal thanks and praise be to you, O blessed God, my Saviour, for all your glorious achievements in laying a sure foundation for our hope and everlasting comfort.

You have loved us and redeemed us and washed us from our sins in your own blood. O how infinitely indebted I am to your mercy that you should call me to such a heavenly state which you purchased and provided for us at so great a price!

O make me more aware of your love and more thankful for all its blessed effects. Let me now find the happy fruits of strength and refreshment for my soul. Let it be strength against all the temptations which would draw me away from you, and refreshment which would render all the pleasures of sin distasteful to me, and make it my primary joy to do the will of my heavenly Father.

After I have experienced the pleasures of my Father's house, O do not let me feed upon what is useless. Let nothing

destroy the sweet desire I have for heavenly things nor let
the world come between me and the blessed Saviour of the
world.

Let me not depart from the Lord who has been so good
and kind to my soul. O let me never rebel against my
heavenly Sovereign to whom I once again have vowed
allegiance.

O blessed Jesus, to whom shall I go? You have the words
and the gift of eternal life. All is in your hands. You are
the best of all lords for you rule us only that you may bless
us. You have commanded us to obey your laws only that
you may keep us from ruining ourselves and secure for us
the highest happiness.

I will admire and love and praise my Lord. I will believe
and trust in his unfailing mercy. I will rejoice and glory in
his great salvation. Who shall pluck me out of his hands?
What shall separate me from his love? My beloved is mine
and I am his. Yours I am, O Lord, and yours I will be while
I live.

Yet, Lord of all power and love, I beseech you to keep
your servant from falling and preserve me during every
occasion of danger. O do not allow me to destroy myself
but pity my frailty and relieve my weakness and infirmity.
In your hands let me be safe and never perish but attain
everlasting life through Jesus Christ, my great Redeemer and
only Saviour. *Amen. Amen.*

4. After

I desire with all my soul to adore and magnify your blessed
name, O Lord God, my heavenly Father, for all the
expressions of your love and bounty to me, a poor unworthy
sinner. I praise you especially for your precious favours and
the renewed pledges of your love in Christ Jesus which I
have received from you this day. For you have admitted me
not only to your house but to your table and treated me as
a friend and one of your family, even me who deserves to

be cast out as an enemy and rejected by you as the most despicable thing in the world.

O what manner of love is this that I should be treated so well when I deserve the opposite from you! O that such should be the case of wretched, sinful men! That the God whom we have greatly offended should not only forgive us but invite us to feast at his table on all which our blessed Saviour has merited and prepared for us!

Lord, what is man that you care for him and the Son of man that you think of him! What am I, one of the most wretched and sinful of men, that the great Lord whom I have so often dishonoured, should deal so very graciously with me? O make me conscious of all that God has freely given to me that I may see the extent of my debt to the Lord for all his kindness to my soul. O give me a heart that is deeply aware of your mercy and steadfastly determines to live to your glory, that I may show my thankfulness for your benefits by my obedience to your commands. Let me remember always the obligations laid upon me and help me to live as one who has his holy Redeemer dwelling in him.

As I have received Christ Jesus the Lord, so help me to walk in him as a worthy servant and pleasing to all. Enable me to love as Christ has loved us and to continue in the strength which I have received from you, pursuing holiness and perfecting it in godly fear.

As I have eaten and drunk of the sacramental bread and wine for the nourishment and refreshment of my frail body, so let the body and blood of God my Saviour nourish and sustain my immortal soul unto eternal life.

O that the sacrifice of Christ Jesus, that sacrifice of himself which he offered upon the cross, and which I have this day been commemorating at your table, may atone for all the failings and defects of my preparation and reception. As a result of his great atonement for the sins of the whole world, may I be pardoned and accepted by you, my God. O grant it I beseech you, through him who loved us and gave himself for us, even the Son of your love, the great lover of our souls, for whom, and to whom, with your eternal self and the Holy Spirit, be ascribed by me and all your Church all thanks and praise, honour and glory now and for ever. *Amen*.

(vii) Three prayers for the Church

1

O God of all grace, you have called out of this present evil world a chosen people to know your will, to seek your face, to follow your ways and to inherit your glory. Pour out your blessings upon those who are still in darkness and the shadow of death: make bare your arm and exert your power throughout all the earth so that its inhabitants may recall their true identity and turn to the Lord: then all flesh shall see the salvation of God.

Call to yourself your once favoured people the Jews: take the veil from their eyes that they may see and accept their Messiah. Let that blood of Christ, which they invoked upon their own heads, cleanse them from the guilt of shedding it: let the blood cleanse them from all their sins.

Bring in, also, O God, the fulness of the Gentiles, and give to your Son the nations for his inheritance and the ends of the earth for his possession. O give the Gospel a free and effective passage throughout the world. Let it be proclaimed where it has not yet reached and let the joyful sound be heard even where Christ is not yet named. Give success to it where it shines already: let all who have received it sincerely obey it; cause every one that names the name of Christ to depart from evil; and grant that all who make a profession of godliness may be constrained by the love of Christ to live unto you and to adorn the doctrine of God our Saviour in all things.

Convince and convert both the avowed enemies of Christ and also the enemies of his house. Beat down all antichristian powers both in the false church, where Christianity is so corrupted, and also beyond the borders of Christendom, where it is openly opposed. Reveal unto all of them the light of your truth that they may know it as it is in Jesus. Expel their prejudices together with their darkness and bring them to receive your truth and to love it that they may be saved.

O that the true religion of our Lord Jesus may powerfully prevail and gain more converts daily throughout the world. O that Jerusalem may soon become the joy and praise of the whole earth and that we may see the good of it all the days of our life!

O Father of lights, grant that all errors in doctrine and all ungodly practices may be exposed and suppressed until they are completely abolished! Let the wickedness of the wicked come to an end; but, let truth and holiness increase in credit and authority until they reign and flourish even to the ends of the earth: grant this, we most humbly ask, through the abundant grace of our Lord Jesus Christ. *Amen.*

2

Blessed be your name, O Lord our God, for you have called us to be your people. You have caused the rising sun to come down to us from heaven to visit us and the light of your gospel to shine upon us in our darkness. You have sent to us the Word of salvation and made your holy Faith to be our birthright and the professed religion of our nation.

You have not been lacking in kindness to us, O gracious Lord, but how grievously have we failed in our duty to you! You have done great things on our behalf but how little have we done in your service and how much have we gone against your holy, good and righteous laws! As the vineyard of the Lord, we have experienced your care and kindness for a long time; you have surrounded us with your providence, pruned us by your judgements, and watered and refreshed us by your mercies. Therefore, in justice, you might expect to find in us fruit worthy of your care.

But, alas! We have produced wild grapes and have been overgrown with briers and thorns of contention. Too often our good works have been no better than the unfruitful works of darkness. We confess, O Lord, that we have walked unworthy of our holy calling and that you might in justice take away the Gospel from us, and give it to another people who will produce fruits more worthy of it.

But, O gracious, long-suffering God, who in judgement have always remembered mercy towards us, enter not into judgement with us for our neglect of you. Do not count against us the guilt of the numerous evils of which our consciences accuse us − our lack of response to all the means of grace, our ingratitude for your most precious blessings and our abuse of the numberless favours which we have enjoyed for so long.

Do not remember our sins against us, but remember your own tender mercies and loving-kindnesses, which we have long known. Do not say to this land that you have no pleasure in it, but return, we beg you, O God of hosts: look down from heaven to behold and then to visit this vineyard and the branch which you made strong for yourself. Be as a wall of fire around our Church to protect it against all that would invade its peace, corrupt its purity or destroy its prosperity. Be in the middle of us as a refiner's fire and like a launderer's soap to purge away our dross and to purify us more and more from all our remaining errors and corruptions. Let your Church be established at the centre of the nation: let righteousness be the foundation of her walls and peace the ornament of her palaces.

O may your right hand which is lifted high and has done mighty things work wonders for our safety. Be pleased, O Lord, to create such a holy reformation among us that we may not be nominally but really a reformed people, even a people belonging to God, who are zealous to do good works. Make us eminent for that righteousness which exalts a nation in order that you, the righteous Lord, who love righteousness, may bless us and protect us with your favour.

You have seen how much we have previously resisted the means you have used for our good, but be merciful unto us and cause your anger towards us to cease. Rejoice over us to do good to us for you know what will be effective to reclaim and save us. Give us grace that will both be sufficient for us and effectively persuade us to walk worthily in the vocation to which you have called us. Do not reject our prayer but hear and answer us, O God of our salvation, for the sake of Jesus Christ, your Son, our Lord. *Amen*.

3

O Lord most high, you are the glorious head of all the Church! You have appointed various officers in it for the perfecting of the saints, for the work of the ministry, for the edifying of the body of Christ. Bless in a special way all those whom you have sent to bless your people in your name: make all our spiritual fathers careful and tender nursing fathers of your Church. Grant them both knowledge and grace that they may conduct their lives as they ought.

Enable them to care for souls, to feed the flock of God and to take the oversight of it heartily and willingly and without looking for financial reward. May they care for all people committed to their charge, providing what each person truly needs. Enable them rightly to interpret your Word and to proclaim it effectively, that they may be useful to their contemporaries and gain your approval as workmen who need not be ashamed of their work.

Make them skilful and faithful in their holy callings, and in all their attempts to promote the knowledge and love of your truth, give them good success. Let their example and teaching be such as shall both help to save themselves and those that hear them.

O that they may speak as the oracles of God with a demonstration of the Spirit's power and that they may prove themselves to be examples of all the good things they preach to others. Let them not prostitute their calling to serve the interests and lusts of men but rather conscientiously discharge it to the glory of their Lord! Let them not use deception or handle the Word of God deceitfully; but by setting forth the truth plainly may they commend themselves to every man's conscience in the sight of God. Let them be such examples to the flock that having preached to others they themselves may not be disqualified for the heavenly prize, but may experience the joy of that salvation which they preach. And when the chief Shepherd shall appear may they be counted worthy to receive the crown of glory which does not fade.

Though the world hates and the devil opposes them and even many who should encourage them actually hinder and afflict them, do you, O great and good Lord, reveal your strength to accomplish your work. Open a wide door for the Gospel and defeat all opposition. Close the mouths of false prophets and drive away ravenous wolves from the flock: instead, provide faithful pastors with hearts like yours.

O Lord, crown the work of your messengers with your heavenly blessing so that they may be mighty through God to pull down strongholds of sin and to edify and build up your Church in the true fear and love of God and in the right knowledge and faith of our Lord Jesus Christ. Because wise men die and cannot bequeath their learning and talents unto others, intervene to supply the vacancies caused by their deaths. Bless our universities and all the schools and seminaries of sound learning and true religion in the land that they may send forth men able and fit to serve you in Church and State. May they do good in their generations and show your people the way of happiness and salvation. *Amen.*

4

PRAYERS FOR USE ON CHURCH FESTIVALS

(i) Introduction

Being faithful and convinced ministers of the Church of England, both Jenks and Simeon only kept those festivals and saints' days (normally for apostles) for which provision was made in the Book of Common Prayer. They were not interested in celebrating the extended list of saints' days of the medieval Catholic or the modern Roman Catholic Churches. However, neither were they Puritans who rejected all holy days except Sundays. So they celebrated enthusiastically Christmas, Good Friday, Easter Sunday, Ascension Day and Whitsuntide (Pentecost) together with the other special days required by the B.C.P. Each of these festivals provided opportunity to celebrate an aspect of the great salvation provided by God the Father through Jesus Christ, the Son, in the power of the Holy Spirit.

(ii) Six prayers from Christmas to Saints' Days

1. The Incarnation: Christmas

Blessing and honour and glory and power be to him who sits upon the throne and to the Lamb for ever and ever! O Lord God of our salvation! You have remembered us in our great need; you have raised up a great salvation and a mighty deliverance for us; you have sent your only begotten Son to heal the sinful, to help the miserable and to save the lost.

None but you, O Lord, knows the greatness of that gift which you have conferred upon us − the greatest that you could give, or man receive. None can duly estimate your mercy in giving your only Son to be our mighty Saviour, to deliver us from the miseries of hell, and to exalt us to the thrones of glory.

O how wonderful have been the designs of your love, and the counsels of your wisdom! That you should recover our lost souls and work for them a salvation so worthy of yourself! That the eternal Word should be manifested in the flesh to destroy the works of the devil! That the eternally beloved Son should be made the Son of man in order that we might become the children of God!

O what manner of love has the Father bestowed upon us! How infinitely does it exceed all that we can ever say of it! O that all might praise you, O Lord, for your goodness and for your wonderful works unto the human race! O that we, in particular, might receive this great mystery of godliness with the deepest reverence and most lively gratitude! Let our souls magnify the Lord, and our spirits rejoice in God our Saviour. Yes, forever blessed be the Lord God of Israel, that he has visited and redeemed his people.

Now that you have laid help for us upon One that is mighty and found in him a ransom for us, O help us, blessed God, to receive and welcome the joyful news that Jesus Christ is come into the world to save sinners. Father of mercies! Prepare our hearts to embrace your inestimable gift. Let him who came into the world in the fulness of time, now come into our souls in the fulness of his grace. Let him who was miraculously formed in the virgin's womb, be spiritually formed in our hearts now.

O great Lord and lover of souls! Remember us with the favour which you bear to your people and visit us with the joy of your salvation. O make the way of salvation plain to us that we may know where our help lies and what we must do to be saved. Incline and strengthen us, O Lord, to comply with the gracious designs of your mercy and to receive with all thankfulness your grace which brings us salvation.

O blessed Saviour, be a real Saviour unto us. Save us from our sins that you may also save us from the wrath to come. Redeem us from all iniquity that you may also redeem us from everlasting misery. You came down to earth to raise us up to heaven. You took our nature that we might partake of yours. O let us then experience the mighty power of your grace! Let it heal our depraved natures, let it sanctify our sinful souls, and let it make us lovers and followers of your holy ways. Let those good things which accompany salvation be multiplied unto us exceedingly through the knowledge of our incarnate Lord.

Let the great and wonderful things which you have done for us in revealing your salvation and in opening a door of hope to us, dwell richly in our minds. Let a sense of your infinite loving-kindness ever constrain us to love and serve you with all our heart and mind and soul and strength, O God our Father, for your dear Son's sake. To him, together with your blessed self and the Holy Spirit, Three Persons in one glorious Godhead, be equal and everlasting glory. *Amen*.

2. The Death of Jesus: Good Friday

O God, the Father of mercies, and of our Lord Jesus Christ, through whom every mercy is conferred and channelled to us, you created us in your own blessed image in a holy and happy state. We have defaced the work of your hands and have brought ourselves into a state of alienation from you and of enmity against you. Yet you have not dealt with us as enemies or left us in the sad ruins of our fall. You have pitied us and urged us to live. You have even given your only begotten Son to die for us to save us from that everlasting death, which is the just wages of our sins.

O most holy Lord God, you spared him not, that you might spare us and make us eternal examples of your saving mercy. O what amazing, unspeakable love is this, that, even when enemies, we should be reconciled to God by the death of his Son! But O the cursed nature of sin that needed such an atonement; the inexorable justice of my God that required it, and the incomprehensible love of my Saviour who offered it upon the cross!

O that we could always remember these things! That we could hate sin with a perfect hatred! That we could stand in awe of our God, and fear to offend him! That we could love that adorable Saviour, who bought us at the inestimable price of his own blood!

Most blessed God, we desire to bless and magnify your name for revealing to us this stupendous mystery. By it we abide, and upon it we depend, for the pardon of our sins and for our whole acceptance with you both here and in eternity. We believe, O God, that your dear Son has fully discharged our debt and that nothing at all remains to be paid by them, for whom you are pleased to accept his infinite satisfaction.

Seeing that there is balm in Gilead, and a physician that is able to heal us, O let not our souls be unhealed. Let not the great things which our Lord Redeemer has done and endured for perishing sinners be lost to us. Let the same be mercifully accepted upon our account, as the payment of our debt. O let not the blood of Jesus Christ be shed in vain. Let it purge and purify us from all our sins and make our peace with you against whom we have so greatly transgressed. Let us be healed by his stripes and find through his death an opening for us into new life.

Though we are sinful and unclean, this precious fountain, opened for sin and uncleanness, can wash and cleanse us from all pollution and defilement. As we have such an all-sufficient Saviour to go to, let us not be faithless, but truly believe that Christ is our Lord and our God who loved and redeemed us, and washed us from our sins in his own blood. O that we may know him and the fellowship of his sufferings, and become like him in death. Let the cross of Christ be the means of crucifying the world unto us and us unto the world.

Pardon, O good Lord, all our forgetfulness of you and make us to know more of the love with which you have loved us. Touch our hearts with such a wonderful sense of your love that we may make better responses in love to you who have done such great things for our souls. Let us never forget or slight such unparalleled kindness but be constrained by it to live unto him who died for us and rose again. O that the life that we now live may be by the faith of the Son of God, who loved us and gave himself for us! Let us more and more abound in your love.

Blessed Lord! Let the serving and enjoying of you be ever preferred above our chief earthly joy. Let nothing in the world ever be so dear to us as the name of our adorable Emmanuel who has given the greatest demonstration of love that ever could be given to our perishing souls. For what you have done for us, be all possible glory and honour and praise ascribed to you, O most blessed Saviour and Redeemer, by all the people of God, both now and for evermore. *Amen.*

3. The Resurrection: Easter Sunday

Blessed be the God and Father of our Lord Jesus Christ, who, according to his abundant mercy, has given us a new birth into a living hope, by the resurrection of Jesus Christ from the dead. Blessed be Jesus, who lives and was dead; and, behold, he is alive for evermore, Amen. He has the keys of death and of hell. The Lord lives! Blessed be our rock, and let the God of our salvation be exalted. He has borne our griefs, and carried our sorrows. He has gained eternal salvation for us; with his own right hand and holy arm he has been victorious: and God, the Father, set him free from the agony of death because it was impossible for death to keep its hold on him. We adore the glorious sun of righteousness who is risen with healing in his wings: he has showed that he is able to save himself, and to save to the uttermost all those who come to God through him.

Our eyes gaze upon you, O Lord, our life, our strength and our Redeemer, who possess all power in heaven and on earth. To you nothing is impossible or difficult: you give new life to the dead, both to souls dead in sin and bodies dead in the grave. You have life in yourself to give to whom you choose. O that we may know you, and the power of your resurrection! May your power raise us out of the grave of our corruptions to newness and holiness of life; that having a part in the first resurrection, we may never be subject to the second death.

Speak death to our sins, O Lord, that our souls may live and for ever bless your name. You, O Christ, are our life; and in you is the fulness of all we can possibly want: O give us the life, which you came to impart: and let us have it in abundance. Let us have such life from you as may enable us to live unto you entirely and cheerfully all our days. *Amen.*

4. The Ascension: Ascension Day

You are the King of glory, O Christ: you have ascended on high, and led captives in your train, dragging your vanquished enemies behind your triumphant chariot. You are exalted far above all principalities and powers and enthroned in the highest glory of your kingdom, where saints and angels, even all the host of heaven, admire and adore you. Be exalted, O Lord, and reign in the greatness of your power and majesty until you have brought all your enemies under your feet.

Lord, remember us, now that you are in your kingdom. O pay attention to the supplications and relieve the needs of your poor servants here below. Save, Lord, and let the King of heaven hear us when we call. And, O that we may feel the powerful attraction of your grace to draw up our minds and desires from the perishable enjoyments of this world to those unspeakable and everlasting glories above, where you sit at the right hand of the Father. O let us lay up our treasure, and have our true home with you, in heaven; may we so love your appearing, as to be ever looking for and hastening to the coming of that blessed day, when we shall lose our mortal bodies and be with Christ in our resurrection bodies; for when Christ who is our life shall appear, we also shall appear with him in glory.

Enable us now, we pray, to ascend and dwell with you in the constant exercise of faith and love so that on the last day we may personally ascend in soul and body to be for ever with the Lord: and there, together with your whole, triumphant Church, to see and admire, to love and bless, to praise and glorify you, O blessed God our Saviour, world without end. *Amen.*

5. *The Descent of the Holy Spirit: Pentecost*

O infinite, eternal Spirit, the Lord and giver of life, who works in all things, but especially in the souls of men; pardon all the guilt we have contracted in resisting your movements and quenching the flames you have kindled in our hearts. Be pleased so to enlighten our minds and purify our hearts, that we may be ready to receive and entertain you as the guide and comforter of our souls.

O Spirit of truth, lead us into all truth. Bring all needful things out of the Word into our memories, and place them powerfully upon our hearts, to influence our lives and to do us good in every time of need. Whatever grace is lacking in us, form it in our hearts as you establish and increase what you have already created in us. Stir us up to desire all that is good and enable us both to perform it as well as to continue and persist in it.

O come down, Lord, as fire upon us to consume our dross and to make our hearts clean. Set them on fire with heavenly love that we may devoutly relish holy things and be lively in following your holy ways. Be a powerful principle of life, light and love as well as of all grace and holiness in our souls: illuminate our minds; make our affections spiritual; pacify our consciences and bring our souls out of every dangerous, self-destroying course into the paths of righteousness.

O blessed Lord Jesus, restrain us from grieving the Holy Spirit, by whom we are sealed until the day of our redemption. Do not cast us away from your presence and take not your Holy Spirit from us. O make us submissive to his holy movements that we may experience his heavenly comfort and consolations. May the joy of the Holy Spirit be more to us than all the pleasures of the world.

O blessed Spirit be with our spirits to heal our disturbed minds and heal our infirmities; work mightily upon our hearts by your grace until our souls are fitted for that glory which is unspeakable and everlasting. *Amen.*

6. The Commemoration of an Apostle or Saint

O God of all grace, you are pleased to call out of this present world an elect people for yourself and to pour out your Spirit upon them; you make them shine as lights within a warped and crooked generation to be examples to the rest of mankind. We bless your holy name that you have not left us destitute of such models which serve to show us the nature of our duties and provide us with encouragement to perform them. Inspire us, we pray, to take that excellent way in which they (with such happy success) have gone before us. Constrain us to become followers of them as they were of Christ.

Seeing that we are surrounded with so great a cloud of witnesses, enable us, we pray, to throw away everything that hinders and the sin that so easily entangles, in order to run with perseverance the race marked out for us! Teach us and strengthen us, O King of saints, to make a profitable use of those gifts and graces whereby your faithful servants adorned their holy vocation; and so to imitate their virtues as to convince the world that the righteous person is indeed more excellent than his unrighteous neighbour.

O that we may never persecute your saints nor despise

those who are as the apple of your eye — whose great concern is to stay faithful in your covenant and be zealous for your glory. May we ever hold such in the highest reputation whilst they are alive that we count their memories precious when they are dead. O heavenly Father, let them be dearest to us who are dearest to yourself. Let our delight be in the saints that are on earth — of whom the world in abusing them is not worthy of them.

O let us not be conformed to this world, nor follow the majority to do evil, but be followers of those who through faith and patience do already inherit your glorious promises. May we so live the life of the righteous that we may also die their death. Help us, O Lord our God, so to imitate your saints here in their holiness that hereafter we may be numbered with them in everlasting glory. As we desire and hope for a share in their blessed end, O let us love and follow their godly way. And make the communion of saints to be that experience which we desire, as well as an article of the creed we believe.

Let us be lovers of all good people, honouring them that fear the Lord, and regarding them very highly in love for what they are and do. O Lord, increase the number of your faithful people in all places and add daily to the Church those who shall be true followers of God, as dear children. Let your kingdom come, and your will be done on earth as it is in heaven; let your Church grow and flourish, until we, with all your servants departed in the Lord, meet together in the kingdom of our Father, to live in your presence, and to enjoy your love and to glorify your name, world without end. *Amen*.

5

PERSONAL PETITIONS FOR GROWTH IN SPIRITUALITY

(i) Introduction

In these petitionary prayers we gain important insights into the evangelical Anglican and moderate Calvinist piety commended by Jenks and Simeon. It is an authentically biblical piety which is rooted in the psalter (which they read/prayed through each month) and the New Testament in particular, but is also informed by the great prophetical books of the Old Testament. It is also a demanding piety which takes personal sin extremely seriously and thus has high views of the atoning blood of Christ and the sanctifying work of the Holy Spirit. There is also great emphasis upon both (a) the absolute requirement to be practical and to reveal the Gospel by good behaviour and loving action and (b) the important duty to be heavenly-minded and prepared to meet the Lord at any time.

Perhaps the best way to use these prayers is to read them carefully and ask what they can add to our prayers. What do they have in terms of ethos and content which our prayers do not have? Having discovered this and being persuaded that what they have is valuable it will be appropriate to ask how these insights can be added to our prayers. What will probably stand out as different from contemporary prayers is the profound estimate that is taken of sin and of God's hatred of it (of sin, not the sinner).

But another way is to use them for meditatory prayer — that is to read them very slowly, apply their content to oneself, and then turn the words into an actual personal prayer.

(ii) Personal Prayers for the grace of God

1. For illumination and knowledge

O Lord God, eternal, uncreated light, you have not left yourself without witness amongst us. In your Word and works before us, in our souls and consciences within us, and in all your creatures on every side of us, you have left traces of your power, wisdom and goodness. Therefore it is to my shame that I do not have a better knowledge of you as the Saviour and of how I may be in a right relationship with you. It is entirely because of my spiritual dulness and negligence that I have made no progress in receiving your revelation. O Lord, I have not improved in my knowledge of you in proportion to the light which you have caused to shine upon me, nor according to the means of instruction with which you have blessed me. Further, I have need to be taught myself the very things of which I might have been a teacher of others. For these sins I desire, O Lord, to humble myself before you and to implore your pardon: and further I now come to ask wisdom at your hands, knowing that you give generously to all, without reproaching.

I cannot see or know you, O Lord, except by the beams of your own light which you are pleased to impart. I ask, O Lord, that you will continue graciously to reveal yourself more fully to my soul. Teach me to know you aright, the only true God, and Jesus Christ whom you have sent. O blessed sun of righteousness, arise upon me with healing in your wings to scatter all the clouds of folly and ignorance, error and prejudice which cover my soul.

Open my eyes that I may see wonderful things in your Law. Open my understanding that I may understand the

Scriptures and not remain in darkness concerning anything I need to know both for my present peace and duty and for my eternal safety and happiness. And whenever I — or anyone for whom I have responsibility — act contrary to what we ought to do, reveal the same to us, O God. In fact, let all of us, whatever our age or position, be taught by you both to love you and to know what your will for us is.

It is not good that the human soul should be without knowledge. O incline our ears to wisdom and our hearts to understanding, that we may grow to know the Lord and increase in the knowledge of God. Show us your ways, O Lord, and lead us in your truth. Let your Spirit lead us into the mysteries of the kingdom of God. O Lord, you are our light, give us understanding in the way of godliness: give us a spiritual discernment of the things of the Spirit and make us wise unto salvation. Give us the spirit of wisdom and revelation truly to know you; and may the eyes of our understanding be enlightened so that we know the hope to which you have called us, what are the riches of the glory of the inheritance in the saints, and what is the mighty power of your Spirit, who works in them that believe.

O put your revealed Word within us and write it on our hearts so that the Bible may not be to us as a sealed book or a hidden gospel, but rather a lamp to our feet and a light to our paths. O that our ways were directed to keep your statutes! Help us, good Lord, so to do your will that we may know the Scriptures to be divinely inspired and may have the witness of this in our hearts; and may we recognise the divine character of your Word by the power and fruitfulness of it upon our lives.

Now we see but a poor reflection of the divine glory; we know the divine truth only in part; and we cannot fathom the mysteries of God. Yet help us even more and still better to know our God until we shall truly know him as we are now known by him, and enter your presence to see you face to face, and experience fulness of joy for evermore. *Amen.*

2. *For faith and trust in God*

Without faith it is impossible to please you, O God; and therefore I come to ask for a true, living faith, which is your gift. Lord, help my unbelief and increase my faith. Whatever you have revealed let me accept it upon the credit of your Word. Where I have your promise let me not waver through unbelief but fully persuade myself that it shall be as you have said.

O bless and enrich my soul with such a holy, lively and genuine faith as may enlighten my mind, purify my heart, and influence my whole life; give me such a faith as may enable me to receive Jesus Christ for my Saviour and heartily give myself to him as my Lord: so that being ruled and sanctified by him in this life I may be saved and glorified by him eternally in the life that is to come. O help me so to assent to the truths that I may also consent to the terms of the Gospel. Give me that genuine faith which is expressed in love; that faith which will enable me to overcome the world, and to fix my attention on those great and glorious things which are unseen and eternal.

In my greatest darkness and distress, O let me trust in the name of the Lord, and remain close to our God, committing my ways unto you, casting my burden upon you, and putting my trust in you, even though you chastise me. Let me trust in your almighty power to help and to save, and in your tender care to pity and to relieve; and in the sure promises which your love has made good (and which your faithfulness will certainly make good) unto all that wait and call upon you.

And though I do not have answers to all the prayers of my heart, O let me wait patiently for the salvation of the Lord, and keep my eyes upon the Lord my God until you have mercy upon me. Make me so sound and strong in the Faith, that my faith may never fail, but rather be found offering praise and honour and glory in every time of trial; and also at the great appearing of our Lord and Saviour Jesus Christ. *Amen.*

3. For power to live by faith in Christ

It is your command, O my Lord and Saviour, that they who believe in God should believe also in you, as their only Mediator with the Father. Yes, in you, O Christ, who in your Incarnation did not consider equality with God something to be grasped even though you are truly God, blessed for ever. You have told us that to know you is life eternal and that no one can come unto the Father except through you so that no one will perish who believes in you.

O the riches of your grace and the wonders of your mercy that such provision has been made for poor sinners! Blessed be your glorious name for ever and ever! And blessed be the God of all grace who out of his abundant mercy has provided such a remedy for us as lost sinners; we are saved through faith in Christ when we could not be saved by any merits or good works of our own.

Great and holy Lord! I cannot avoid always recognising my need of a Saviour and that I am helpless without your free grace in Christ Jesus. Therefore I desire to go to him, and to be found in him, not having my own righteousness but that which is given through faith in him. I desire to sit down under the shadow of (Christ) that tree of life, which offers the richest fruits, most sweet to all who have ever tasted of his grace.

O that Christ, who is the end of the law for righteousness to every one who believes, may be the Lord, my righteousness; that his righteousness may be imputed to me and with all my heart I may believe unto righteousness! O that I may so believe in Jesus Christ that I may be justified by faith and have peace with God through him!

The blessed Jesus is my life and strength, my wisdom and riches, my health and joy, my glory and my all. There is no healing for my soul but in his precious blood: no peace for my conscience but in his reconciling me to God: no satisfaction to my mind but in that most perfect atonement which satisfied even the strictest justice of heaven. O none but Christ! None but Christ! Without this all-sufficient Redeemer, I am always a lost creature.

Therefore, I earnestly ask you, O Lord, leave me not destitute of him: but make me to participate in Christ, or I die eternally. Though I have slighted all his love for so long and neglected his great salvation continually, yet, O my Father, I dare not add to all my other sins the offence of despairing of that mercy, which, in him, you are pleased to offer even to the most sinful and unworthy. Thus, since you are in Christ Jesus a God reconciling the world to yourself, in that you have given him to be a propitiation for our sins: and since he came to seek and save the lost and to call sinners to repentance; and since he invites to himself all who are weary and burdened – yes, bids all that are thirsty to come and take the water of life freely; and since he promises that he will not cast out any who do come to him, to him I will look and in him I will trust: and, I ask you, heavenly Father, to help me to do what I ought to do.

O be pleased to shine into my heart with your heavenly light to reveal your Son in me and to show me all his all-sufficiency for my needs, yes, to show me also how I may participate in him, in his Body. Dear Lord God, give me your Son to save me and give me your Spirit to draw me to him. Enable me, I pray, to take hold of him, to rely upon him, and to believe in him, to the saving of my soul. O make me more acquainted with the gospel way of saving sinners by Jesus Christ and help me humbly to accept it and thankfully to submit to the righteousness of God in the gospel.

O God of all grace, you justify sinners freely by your grace not for any merit of their works but for the worthiness of your Son, through the redemption that is in Christ Jesus. May I truly believe in him and place my whole trust in him so that, believing, I may have life through his name. May I always be fully persuaded in my own mind that he is the true Messiah, the only Saviour of the world. Let me never distrust his power or his love, never be faithless, but at all times believing and confident that he is my Lord and my God, who loved me and washed me from my sins in his own blood.

May the God of hope fill me with all joy and peace in believing, whilst I lie at the feet of Jesus and cast my burden upon the Lord, and lean on my soul's Beloved. Though there is nothing in me but impurity and disorder, O let me not stay away from my Saviour: but let me come to him at his call, and believe in his name, that through him I may be made clean and whole.

No one more needs your help, O Lord, than I do. O that it may not pass me by: but let the Saviour of the world be the Saviour of my soul; and let Christ abide with my spirit and be always at hand to do me good. O that my Redeemer may look with an eye of favour upon me, and revive me with some tokens of his love, which is better than all the enjoyments and comforts of this world.

Help me, O great Author and Perfector of our faith, to pray in faith, believing that I shall receive the things which I ask in your name. O my Lord and my God, make me to know and believe the love which you have for me — even that you have loved me with an everlasting love. Make me to know in whom I have believed; and that Jesus Christ is my Strength and my Redeemer. Let this sweet, sure hope comfort me through all troubles, fortify me against all temptations, and enable me to perform all my duties. O that Christ may dwell in my heart by faith, and that the life I now live may be by the faith of the Son of God who loved me and gave himself for me: and though I do not see him, yet believing in him, let me rejoice in him with unspeakable joy and glory.

It is your gracious promise, Lord, to blot out your people's transgressions, not to remember their sins and not to let sin have dominion over them. You have promised to have mercy on the wicked and unrighteous and abundantly to pardon them if only they forsake their wicked ways and their unrighteous thoughts. You have assured them that you will take away their heart of stone and give them a heart of flesh: that you will put your Spirit within them, and cause them to walk in your statutes and to keep and do your commandments: and that, when they wholeheartedly commit themselves to you, you will graciously work within them. You have promised that though they fall, you will uphold them with your hand and so put your godly fear in their hearts that they will not finally depart from you. You have assured them that you will preserve them for your heavenly kingdom and give unto them eternal life.

O what exceedingly great and precious promises! What stimulation to fainting souls! For while they are truly great and almost beyond belief they shall all be fulfilled in the fulness of time. God is faithful who promised and he will accomplish what he promised. Your Word is ratified in heaven, O Lord, and not one small part of it shall disappear until all is fulfilled. O let me believe that I, even I, shall see it.

Whenever I am afraid, let me trust in you; and let me give glory to my God, in believing your gracious promises, though I know how unworthy I am to have any part in them. Let me store up your kind words of promise, O my Father, as the richest treasure, and trust in them as the surest heritage – counting nothing so firm as what God himself has said. Finally, in comparison with yourself, and your Son and your Spirit and all your love and your grace and your glory, let me despise all the wealth and honours and pleasures of the world; all of which I earnestly ask of your bountiful hands for the sake of Jesus Christ. *Amen.*

4. For repentance

O most holy God, against whom I have greatly sinned, you are most justly displeased because of my sins! You have revealed your wrath from heaven against all ungodliness and unrighteousness of men, and have declared that unless we repent we shall all perish. You will not save any without repentance, though upon our repentance you have assured us of your gracious pardon and acceptance. When we return to you and humble ourselves before you, you will show us your mercy and grant us your salvation. O gracious Lord, how great is your mercy to bestow upon us this remedy for our sin!

But how averse I am to repent! How unable I am to perform this necessary work! You search hearts and you know that my heart is hardened through the deceitfulness of sin; I cannot humble myself; my heart will always remain hard unless you soften it by your grace. I am no more able to turn to you with my whole heart than I can turn the course of a river back to its original fountain. Unless you draw me; I can never walk in your way; if you do not empower me with power from heaven I must continue for ever a miserable captive of sin and Satan.

Lord, you made water to gush out of the rock, break and melt my stony heart: you created the human heart, take away from me the heart of stone and give me a heart of flesh. Teach me to look on him whom my sins have pierced, and looking, to mourn: cause me to feel bitterly for all the offences I have committed against you, the Lord of love, and the God of all mercies. O give me true repentance for them: such repentance as your holy Word requires and such as your gracious goodness in Christ Jesus will accept: give me that repentance unto life which I shall never regret making.

You know, Lord, that I desire to have that brokenness of heart and that deep contrition which you will not despise. O that you would confer it upon me! O that I might so repent and be converted that my sins might be blotted out and that a period of refreshing might come to me from your presence! Turn me, O good Lord, and I shall be turned. Renew my mind that I may produce fruit appropriate to repentance, not only confessing and lamenting my sins but also hating and forsaking them — yes, hating them in the depths of my soul.

You know, O Lord, that I cannot undo my sins: but, O that I might never repeat them! O that I might have such a sense of your loving-kindness as shall effectively separate me from all my former ways! Let me walk from now on with all possible care and vigilance and make it the great business of my life to keep myself in your fear and love. Let the past, when I did my own will, be left behind. From now on let me have grace to forsake with determination all evil ways and thoughts, so that you may have mercy upon me and abundantly pardon all my many transgressions. Hear me, O God, and answer me, through the infinite riches of your grace and goodness in Christ Jesus, my only Saviour. *Amen.*

5. For humility

O most high God, infinitely glorious above all our highest words and thoughts! You sit enthroned above the circle of the earth and its people are like grasshoppers. Before you all nations are counted as nothing but vanity. O what is man that you, O God, should be so mindful of him and that he should be so unmindful of himself as to overlook his own sinfulness and to be conceited about his own worth and excellence!

I desire, O Lord, to humble myself because of the pride of my heart and to confess with shame that I have thought more highly of myself than I ought to think: I have boastfully set up myself before others when I deserved nothing but shame and ruin. You resist the proud and give grace to the humble: give me the grace of humility. Make me to see what I really am in my sinful nature that I may be accepted in your sight. And cause me, O Lord, to be numbered among those who are poor in spirit, those humble and contrite ones, to whom you will look and with whom you will dwell.

O make me truly aware of my sins and let me know my transgressions that I may not be boastful but look on myself as sinful dust and ashes, deserving only to be rejected and cast out. Let me never accept anything but shame for myself and always give you the glory for whatever good there is in me.

Great and holy God! Make me more zealous to be your child in practice than to rest in being called your child; and also make me better pleased to do my duty than to hear that I have done it. Let me seek not the praise of men but the honour which comes from God alone.

The more I have received from you the more let me render unto you so that I do not have a high opinion of myself but give all the thanks and glory to you for any good which you have caused me to achieve or do. Let me not desire human praise, while I am doing the work of God; but, let me perform all my duties in such a way that I gain the approval of the God who searches and knows the heart.

Grant me so to be aware of my weakness, in my creatureliness and sinfulness, that I may walk humbly with my God and be clothed with his humility. Let me always hate and resist the pride that goes before destruction and so humble myself under your mighty hand that you may exalt me in due time. For all the good that I have ever achieved or enjoyed, to your name and not to mine, be all the praise and glory, humbly and heartily rendered, both now and for evermore. *Amen*.

6. For tenderness of heart

Almighty Lord, the God of all grace, you speak to the heart and it obeys you; who make it soft and gentle when it is callous and hard; and who give sight and sense to those who are blind and past feeling: O show the power of your heavenly grace in working upon this stupid, insensitive heart of mine, that I may know the evil of my sins and what is necessary to bring me into a right relationship with my God. Be pleased to give me such a view of my sins, such humiliation of soul and brokenness of heart as will prepare me for all the promised mercies of my God in Christ Jesus.

O Father of mercies, punish not my past sins by leaving me to continue to desire to commit sin. Never give me up to such blindness of mind and hardness of heart as will render me senseless and beyond correction. But awaken my dull soul into a lively sense of sin, tenderness of conscience, and due understanding of what there is in store for me in eternity. O make me ever watchful over my heart and my ways, that I may continually fear to offend and always endeavour to please my God. Enable me to keep a careful watch over my heart that it does not get hardened through the deceitfulness of sin. Help me to stand at a distance from every evil and accursed thing that provokes your wrath and destroys my soul.

O let me neither continue to sin, that grace may increase, nor abuse the mercy that has so long upheld me and been so abundantly good to me. Give me, O my God, such a rich increase of spiritual life that I shall mature in spiritual sensitivity and understanding. Stimulate my conscience that I may acknowledge my sins and repent of them now so that I do not find myself in that everlasting place where there is no remedy for sin.

From hardness of heart and contempt of your Word and commandments, good Lord, deliver me. Give me a heart that is so soft and tender that it may smite and correct me for even the least evil. Impress it with such a fear of offending you that it may keep me back, not only from gross and scandalous offences, but also from everything that is suspicious, has a tendency to sin, or contains the very appearance of evil. O let me look upon you with child-like tenderness and awe all the days of my life, that I may neither slavishly fear you now nor be consumed with your terrors in the day of your wrath. May I then receive the blessed inheritance of your children, who look and long for the coming of the day of Christ. *Amen.*

7. For godly fear

O Lord the great and dreadful God, in whose hands is my time and at whose mercy is my soul and all that concerns me both here and for ever: you are to be feared, for who may stand in your sight when once you are angry? The fear of the Lord is the beginning of wisdom: thus happy is the man who always fears God. To harden our hearts against your fear is not only folly and impiety but madness and ruin. I am afraid because I have not feared you aright. I am afraid because I have thought so lightly of you who could, if it had pleased you, have treated me as your enemy and cast me at any moment into the depths of hell. I am afraid because I have been so fearless in the ways of sin where I should not have dared to venture. And I have been so timid in the cause of God where I should not have feared the face of any man.

O absolve me, I beseech you, good Lord, from all this guilt that lies upon me. Put your fear into my heart that I may never experience what a dreadful thing it is to fall into the hands of the living God! O stir up my heart to fear your name! Let your fear be ever before my eyes to restrain me from the evil of my ways. Let me so stand in awe of you that I may not dare to provoke you. Let me not be afraid of a mortal man who will die, but of the almighty Lord, the eternal God, who cannot die. Let my fear of loss or suffering (which can at most be only temporal) be as nothing compared with my fear of the sin and wickedness that would deprive me of everlasting good.

O let me fear the Lord and depart from evil. Let me regard my God so highly that I may not wilfully violate his holy laws. Let me always be afraid to dishonour your name or to rebel against your Word or to offer you less than you require at my hands. O that your fear may not only keep down some of my sins, but regulate my whole life, and sway my very heart, that I may do your will entirely from the heart and go on to perfect holiness in the fear of God.

May I fear your name and not dishonour it; fear your wrath and not provoke it; fear your Word and not despise it; fear your goodness and not abuse it; fear your omniscience and not freely commit secret sins; fear your omnipotence and not strive with my Maker on any occasion. Give me, O my God, the right mixture of fear and faith that

I may not become presumptuous or despairing. Grant that if crosses or evils come my way I may not be so shaken that I become unfit to do my duty. May no successes or prospects of this world's good harden my heart or make me rebellious or stubborn towards you. May I regard your glorious Majesty with awe and dutifully respect all your holy commands to the last hour of my life. *Amen.*

8. For the love of God

O God of infinite goodness and love, you are most sweet and amiable in yourself. You are most attractive because of your glorious excellences and perfection and for all the wonders of your mercy and bounty! How rich is your mercy in making us capable of loving you (even the highest angels know no greater bliss). You have not only given us capacities for it, but the greatest obligations to engage our hearts to it!

Yet, despite all the reasons and motives which we have to love our God, O how poor and defective has been my love! In what strangeness and enmity to you, O Lord, have I lived! It is my sin and shame and misery to be so listless and lacking in love towards you. O my God, I have acted foolishly and wickedly in forsaking the spring of living water to dig my own cisterns, broken cisterns, which cannot hold water. I have shut my heart against the love of my chief good and have preferred trifles and vanities of this present time, as well as the satisfaction of my own foolish and hurtful lusts, above you and your love which is better than life itself.

O gracious God, be pleased to pardon all the defects of my love to you and all the excesses of my love to earthly things. Turn my inclinations and affections from all vain objects to your blessed self, who is most worthy of all my love. And – to conquer all my prejudice and win my heart for ever – show yourself to me as a pardoning God, full of compassion, ready to forgive and willing to save. Give me a deeper knowledge of your love for me that I may return a better love to you, the gracious giver of all my good. Touch my heart with such a powerful sense of your loveliness and loving-kindness that I may experience stronger desires and inclinations towards you and greater pleasure and delight in you. May I love all other things as if I did not love them at all, in comparison with my love for you.

May the Lord direct my heart into the love of God and may he pour out and increase love for himself in my heart, that I may love the Lord my God with all my heart and soul and mind and strength. O show me the vanity of all these attractive things which would draw away my love from yourself. So disclose yourself to my soul that my heart may be unalterably fixed on you. Make this heart of mine, which has been so cold and insensitive to your love, to feel from now on your mighty warmth and power. Far from complaining of the want of love, may I come to rejoice in its abundance in my soul.

O my life, my hope, and joy, you have put me eternally under your obligation. Give me the grace and the power to love you. Let me always long to appear before you and delight in the duties which bring me near to you and help me to have communion with you. Increase my love for your Word and for all the things of the Spirit and grace. Let me take more satisfaction and pleasure in the light of your face than in any increase of corn and wine, and all the most desirable enjoyments of this life. O let me not rest in the gifts and forget the bountiful giver of every good thing.

Draw me and join my heart, dear Lord, still nearer to yourself with the cords of love. Together with all my enjoyments in the world, let me enjoy still more of you, my God, in whose enjoyment consists all my life and peace and happiness here and for ever. O my Lord, engage to yourself the chief and choicest affections of my heart and make it the willing captive of your love. Help me at all times to show my love for you by hating evil, keeping your commandments and delighting to do your will. Let the desire of my soul, the care of my heart and the endeavour of my life be to observe and please you. So secure my heart, O Lord, to yourself that I may not depart from you. May I be rooted and grounded in your love and through your help and grace keep myself in the love of God, looking for the mercy of our Lord Jesus Christ unto eternal life. *Amen*.

9. For hope

O Lord God of hope, the blessed Founder of all our great and glorious expectations; you have promised your people such bliss and glory, which is not only above all we deserve to enjoy but above all our very thoughts to conceive. Inconceivable as it is, it is not too great for your almighty hand, and your boundless love, to give. Because you have made such preparations for your people out of your own infinite greatness and goodness, you are not ashamed to be called their God.

No one has seen nor can anyone tell or think the things which you, O God, have in store for them that love you. But it is good for us to hope and quietly wait for the salvation of the Lord. Even in dark days and perilous times when you allow us to know adversity and threaten us with your increasing judgements, it is still our duty patiently to wait for you till you return to us in mercy and cause the light of your face to shine upon us.

O my God, give me such hope as will lift up my head, strengthen my heart, and encourage my spirit against all temptations and discouragements of the present time: grant that I may never yield to any temptations which would destroy my faith and hope or make me unfit for your work and service. O give me the hope of salvation for a helmet, that hope which may be as an anchor to my soul, both sure and steadfast. O let me hope, and praise you more and more, and rejoice in that hope of which I shall never be ashamed; yes, and also hold fast to this hope unto the end!

Though I am sinful and unworthy, let me hope in the Lord with whom there is mercy and full redemption to redeem his people from all their transgressions. O gracious God, infinitely good! My only hope is in your tender mercies and in your exceedingly great and precious promises, which give assurance of pardon and acceptance to all who humbly seek you through the mediation of your Son, Jesus Christ. But I beseech you, O Lord, remember your Word to your servant on which you have caused me to hope. O seal me with that Holy Spirit which is the deposit of our inheritance, that I may abound in hope through the power of the Holy Spirit. Let Christ be in me as my hope of glory, and with this hope help me to purify myself as my Lord is pure, that I may be counted worthy to enjoy you in your kingdom and glory through the name and merits of Jesus Christ, my only Mediator and Redeemer. *Amen.*

10. For charity

O most gracious and merciful Lord our God, you are goodness and love itself; you have commanded that he who loves you should also love his brother: and that we should love our neighbours as ourselves. Father of mercies, forgive me all my sins of uncharitableness. Give me a heart to abound with loving-kindness to all my fellow human beings who are the objects of your fatherly compassion. Let me not despise any for their lowly position nor hate any for their deceitful behaviour nor reject any as condemned because of their scandalous wickedness. Let me be truly affectionate to all, desirous of their holiness and happiness and doing whatever I can to promote it, showing the mercy to others which you know I need, and forgiving others as I myself desire to be forgiven.

Make me ready to distribute and willing to communicate. Just as I should be glad to find favour and find that my wants were supplied, give me, O gracious God, a large heart and as open a hand as I am able, that I may give cheerfully and sow plentifully while I have time, doing good to all men, especially to those who belong to the family of believers. May I love the opportunities of such well-doing and bless your name for giving me a disposition which finds joy in bringing happiness to your children who are poor.

O that we may all show ourselves true disciples of our Lord by the love we have for one another and show that we have passed from death to life because we love our brothers. May we esteem most, and hold dearest to us, those who distinguish themselves in performing your blessed will. O let our love be without hypocrisy, not only in word but in deed and in truth. May we love one another with a pure heart fervently. May we seek the good of all, however undeserving they may be in themselves, or however hostile to us.

Let our delight be in the saints, and in the righteous. Make us to love them as your holy image appears in them, because you have favoured them and have loved them with an everlasting love. O Lord of love, keep me from being over-critical and rash in judging any; grant that I may think and hope for the best which their case merits, and love every one for the sake of him, who has showed the greatest love to us all, even our dearest Lord and only Saviour, Jesus Christ. *Amen.*

11. For chastity

O God of infinite purity, you have called us not to impurity but to holiness. You have commanded us to be holy as you are holy. You have promised that only the pure in heart here will see you in the beauty of holiness and partake of your love there in heaven above. O how shall I, sinful as I am, stand before you in whose sight even heaven itself is not pure! O most gracious Lord, look not upon me as I am in myself for through my sins I have made myself so unworthy that unless you hide your face from my sins you will abhor my soul and pour out all your wrath upon me.

In your tender mercy, wash me thoroughly from my uncleanness. Cleanse me from all my sin and guilt in that fountain opened for sin and for impurity, the precious blood of the Lamb of God who was slain to take away the sins of the world. O Lord, if you are willing, you can make me clean. O create in me a clean heart and say to my defiled soul as you did to the leper, "I am willing; be clean". O my God, cast the impure spirit out of your temple and if he will not go out except by prayer and fasting, let me add such abstinence to my prayers as may help me to mortify the sinful lusts that war against my soul.

By whatever means, help me, O my Strength and Redeemer, to preserve my body in holiness and honour and not in the lusts of sexual desire as if I did not know God. Holy Lord, cast out these lusts that would make your sacrifice ineffective, and drive out these impure temptations which would destroy your grace in my soul. O let me not fulfil the sinful passions of the body lest I die eternally. Enable me by your Spirit to cast away the sinful deeds of the body that I may live forever.

Instead of fulfilling the sinful desires of the body let me hate the very nature which is filled with them and, with utter detestation, not even name the things which others practise without remorse. Help me, my God, to avoid every occasion of falling and to resist every appearance of evil. Help me so to delight in purity and to keep myself from sin that I may walk as a child of my heavenly Father, not grieving your Holy Spirit but doing the things which are pleasing in your sight through Jesus Christ our Lord. *Amen.*

12. For a meek and peaceable character

O Almighty God, you alone can control the unruly wills and affections of sinful men, be pleased to subdue my wild passions and suppress in me that pride which causes contention. Root out every thought that is inconsistent with gentleness and meekness of spirit. O help me to put away all bitterness, wrath, anger, discontent, evil-speaking and all malice. However much I am tempted and provoked, grant that I may be patient and not be overcome by evil, but overcome evil with good. Enable us, O God of patience, to bear one another's burdens and to uphold one another in love that we may strive only for the faith of Christ and to enter in at the narrow gate. May we not provoke one another to evil but to love and good works.

If you, O great God, should enter into judgement with me and break out in fury upon me as I have been when affronted and enraged by my opponents, how soon should I be consumed and sink under the load of my numerous sins! O may I ever dread to show vengeance towards others, knowing how much I myself stand in need of mercy! O God of peace and love, forgive me, I beseech you, all the sins that I have ever committed against peace and love. O let the peace of God rule in my heart and may your wonderful long-suffering towards me ever oblige me to show meekness to all men! Let me bear the ignorance and wickedness, the follies and mistakes, the wrongs and indignities of my fellow men, seeing that I myself am condemned without God's forbearance and have nothing to hope for or to comfort myself in except to find his favour.

O teach and help us all to live in peace, to love in truth, following peace with all men, and walking in love as Christ has loved us, that we may be united and knit together as fellow-members of the same body of which he is the glorious head. Teach me to look at his example who, though grievously wronged and provoked, did not cry, nor rebel, nor cause his voice to be heard in the streets. Let me learn of him meekness and lowliness of heart, that in him I may find rest for my soul. O my God, suppress all bitter resentments in my mind. Let my speech be always kind, and let a meek and quiet spirit express itself in the way I conduct my life. Lord, make us all gentle and peaceable, easy to be approached and hard to be provoked that we may follow God as dear children. And I pray that you, the God of peace, may be with us, may delight to dwell among us and rejoice over us to bless us; for your mercy's sake in Christ Jesus. *Amen.*

13. For patience

O my God, you know what an evil world we live in and how much I myself have contributed to make it still worse by my sins. Shall I, who have done so little good and so much evil, expect nothing but good at your hands? You have told us that in the world we shall have adversities. O that adversity may create patience in me and that I may be contented to bear whatever you are pleased to lay upon me. Help me to remain patient however tested by your corrections or by men's injuries. To blame the means or complain of your providence for the pressures I am under is only to torment myself and add to that which I already find grievous to endure. O help me to find a better way to ease my sufferings and do my duty than to disturb my peace with vain complaining.

Whatever you do to me, O Lord, let me be dumb and not open my mouth to reply or murmur, because it is your doing. Make me to submit and rest satisfied even in the bitterest ordering of your good providence; also make me contented with what I have and reconciled to what I lack. Since I deserve nothing but trouble and sorrow, let me not be complaining and disobedient: cause me to realise that you do not punish or reward me as my sins deserve. May I patiently encounter all difficulties and grievances in my pilgrimage through this demanding and difficult world, knowing that the same afflictions are endured by others and that they are the common lot of all sinful humanity.

O make me patient until the coming of the Lord, enduring all things with a meek and quiet spirit, thoroughly convinced that they who endure are happy and that those who endure to the end will be saved. O my Lord, let not any pains or sufferings ever drive me from you but rather be the means of bringing me nearer to you. Let the knowledge of the great day of the Lord, and of the eternal state that is approaching, create in me contempt of this world's pleasures, a suppression of my lusts, and patient endurance of the cross. Make me to feel that it is of very little importance what we enjoy or what we suffer here for a short period, provided we are delivered from the wrath to come and are happy in your kingdom for ever. O let me by patient continuance in well-doing seek for glory, honour, and immortality, and count nothing in this world either dear to possess or difficult to suffer, so that I may complete my pilgrimage with joy and, at the last, rest from all my labours and troubles, with the redeemed and blessed of the Lord. All this I wait and ask for at your good hands, O my gracious Father, for the sake of Jesus Christ. *Amen.*

14. *For the mortifying of sinful desires*

I have heartily promised you, my God, to renounce all the desires of my sinful nature for I am consecrated to the Lord. Having been clothed with the Lord Jesus Christ by faith, I should not think how to gratify the desires of my sinful nature, but should cleanse myself from all sin and grow in holiness and in the fear of God. For in my inner being I delight in God's law; but I see another law at work within me, waging war against the law of my mind and making me a prisoner of the law of sin at work within me. This I acknowledge and freely confess before you, O Lord, my God, who alone can set me free from the lusts that are too strong for me to subdue. Help me, O God of my salvation, against the power of these prevailing sins and purge away my sins for the glory of your name.

Let the period in which I served my own lusts and pleasures come to an end. O let not sin any longer reign in my mortal body that I should obey its lusts. But help me, Lord, to cut off the right hand, to pluck out the right eye, and to keep my body under subjection that I may master my lusts and overcome the sins that have so often overcome me. O kill and destroy in me every vicious inclination that exalts itself against your authority and gives Satan an advantage over me.

Preserve me, Lord most holy, from all those sinful pleasures which would rob me of the pleasures which flow from you. O let me not lead a sensual life, minding the sinful inclinations of the flesh as if they were worthy of my esteem. Make me spiritually-minded, that I may, above all things, taste and delight in the things of the Spirit of God. Let not any sinful appetite but only your heavenly Spirit and grace be dominant in my soul. You, and you alone, O my God, govern my heart and life. Let the sins to which I am most strongly tempted especially be effectually subdued. Let me not yield myself a miserable slave to my lusts but conduct myself as a wise and faithful follower of my Lord and Saviour.

As you, O God, who called me, are holy, so make me holy in my whole being and way of life that, being a lover and follower of holiness, I may be counted worthy to see and enjoy my Lord. Make me mighty in the spiritual conflict in which I am engaged. Enable me to fight against those internal foes who are too strong for me to fight alone, that through Christ strengthening me I may conquer all obstructions to your glory and my salvation. May I go on by your grace conquering and to conquer till Satan be for ever defeated. Fight for me, and fight with me, O my God, that nothing may ever separate me from your love which is in Christ Jesus my Lord. *Amen.*

15. For sincerity

O my Lord, the only wise God, whose understanding is infinite and to whom all thoughts are known, you fill the whole world with your presence and nothing can be hidden from your sight. You are the source of knowledge and you know everything. You search the heart and know even our most secret sins. You require truth in our innermost being for you will bring every work, every secret thing, whether good or evil, into judgement.

My God, I acknowledge and readily confess the guile and deceitfulness of my heart. I am deeply sorry that I have been so unmindful of your presence and so inattentive to your glorious Majesty. I confess, Lord, that for this you could have relegated me to the fate of hypocrites. But as you have spared me, humble me, I beseech you, and pardon me for all the hypocrisy and treacherous dealings of which I have been guilty. As you can speak to the heart and order it as you will, create in me a clean and pure heart so that I may not be ashamed or be found lacking in that day when you shall come to judge the world.

O let your all-seeing eye, and not the eye of the world, restrain and regulate my conduct. Let your blessed favour more than the approval of sinful man, ever be the source of my study and delight. Search me, O God, and test me and whatever unpardoned guilt or unrepented wickedness, whatever unknown error or favoured lust lies in my soul, O help me to see it, and of your mercy deliver me from it, and let me not harbour iniquity in my heart. Let no presumptuous sins have dominion over me. Deliver me from the way of wickedness and from serving you with formality and hypocrisy, and enable me to walk before you with an upright heart and do all things sincerely and heartily as unto the Lord.

O let me be a complete Christian and not one who is only almost one. Let me obey from the heart all your holy will, and not be so concerned to seem religious as to be so in deed and in truth. Make me willing to part with the dearest sins, and to perform the hardest duties, for the sake of that adorable Saviour who left the highest glory and endured the worst misery for the sake of my soul.

O make me true to my own convictions and faithful in executing my duties. Make me keep a watchful eye over my heart and be conscientious in all my thoughts, words and ways, that I may not gain the approval of men but that of God; and may I continually rejoice in having a pure conscience and that internal peace of God which passes all understanding. O my Father, who sees in secret, let the obeying of your holy will, the honouring of your blessed name and the enjoyment of your gracious favour be the great end which I design and aim at in all my actions and undertakings so that you, the great and good God, may in all things be glorified by me through Jesus Christ. *Amen.*

16. For a submissive spirit before God

O my great and glorious Maker and Redeemer, my continual Preserver, my only Lord and Owner, I am yours in every way by all the ties of duty and love. I am not at my own disposal for you have formed me for yourself and ransomed me at great cost, after I had given myself over to sin. I have been solemnly devoted to you and have vowed to renounce all tempters that would rival my blessed Lord and to serve you, my God, and to walk in your holy ways, all the days of my life. Nor is this a matter only of duty and obligation but it is my honour and interest, my highest perfection and my greatest bliss.

With confusion and remorse I must acknowledge, O Lord, that I have profanely alienated myself from you and most foolishly and wickedly forsaken you to serve other lords. I have allowed myself to be under the power and servitude of my own vain feelings and sinful passions, not so much concerned to honour you as to please myself, as if I were altogether my own, and had no Lord over me. O my God, forgive and mortify in me this wicked and pernicious selfishness. Let me no longer unjustly withhold myself from you nor madly expose myself to ruin, by living in the world without you.

May I not vainly hope to unite the incompatible service of both God and mammon. Make me so mindful both of my duty and happiness that willingly and cheerfully I may devote myself to the blessed Author of my being, so that I may both answer the purpose for which I was made and also attain the happiness of which I am capable. Seeing I have no sufficiency in myself but derive all my good from union with my God, I am convinced, O Lord, that I ought to yield up myself to you by my own free choice and voluntary act. O bring me to this surrender of myself to you and make me faithful and wholehearted in doing it.

My Lord, break all the ties that separate me from you.

Keep and cause me to continue in your fear and love to my life's end. Upon my mind and memory, upon my will and affections, upon my heart and conscience, write "Holiness to the Lord", and in every way make me willing to be wholly yours. Let your will ever be a law to me in all things and melt down my stubborn will so that it readily agrees with your holy pleasure.

O let me love what you love and hate what you hate. Let my soul and body, with all their faculties and powers, be under your control and employed to your glory. Let all that I am, and all that I have, be truly yours in deed and truth. Never let me think it hard to renounce all for my God, who is infinitely better to me than ten thousand worlds. O help me so sincerely to deny myself that I may own no guide and ruler but my great Lord and Governor. May my eyes ever look towards you and my whole self entirely depend upon you, that in all things you may ever be glorified by me through Jesus Christ. *Amen.*

17. For increase of grace

O God of all grace, you bring the dead back to life and are the Author and perfector of our faith; you have told us that the path of the righteous is as the shining light which shines more and more until the perfect day and that they go from strength to strength, growing in grace, till they appear before you in glory. But O, Lord, how barren and unfruitful have I been among such stalwarts of righteousness; how little profit have I shown under all the means of grace which you have mercifully bestowed upon me; how weak and low is my spiritual state; how weak is my will and strength to do that which is good; how much less am I than many of your servants who have not had the helps and advantages which I have so long enjoyed; and how little evidence there is in my life of the great things the Lord has done in my life!

O my God, I have not made good use of the talents which

you have kindly given to me nor returned the care and kindness of heaven which I have so long experienced. You have denied me nothing, O good Lord, but I have exceedingly failed in my duty to you and myself. I am ashamed that it is no better with me and that so many mercies have been lost upon me. Forgive me, O my Father, and renew your blessed image in me. O help me more and more to put off the old self which is corrupt because of its deceitful desires and to put on the new self which is created by God to be righteous and holy. Whatever else I lack, do not, O Lord, deny me your grace; but, increase it in me and reveal it more and more to me. Yes, let the graces of your spirit which accompany salvation, so flourish in my soul that the peace of God which passes all understanding may keep my heart and mind through Jesus Christ.

Blessed Saviour, who came into the world that we might have life, and have it more abundantly, let me receive out of your fulness sufficient grace that I may be strong in the Lord and ready for every good work. My Life, my Strength and my Redeemer, do not leave me under the curse of unfruitfulness to stand still or backslide in spirituality. But, as you have accomplished any good works through me, establish me in your grace and strengthen me therein, I beg you, lest I die a spiritual death. Let the seed of grace which you have sown in my heart be watered by your good Spirit, that my soul may prosper and increase through your gracious care even as a watered garden, or as a spring whose waters do not fail. Make me to grow in knowledge and in grace and to abound in all those fruits of righteousness which, by Christ Jesus, are to the praise and glory of God so that I may know that I am your servant.

O my Lord, carry on with power the work of faith and holiness in my soul that my sinful corruption may grow weaker and weaker and your grace in me may grow stronger and stronger until, after groaning in the body of sin and death, I come to triumph over the enemies of my soul. O give me constant supplies of your grace so that the means of grace which you are pleased to provide for me may not be wasted; but that in using them, I may be made even wiser, holier, better and more fitted for your blessed acceptance in Jesus Christ, my only Saviour. *Amen.*

18. For inner renewal

I acknowledge and lament before you, O living and all-seeing God, my sinful dulness and laziness in my duties of your holy service. When I should delight in the law of God and serve you with gladness and make it my sole object to do the will of my heavenly Father, O how cold and unwilling I am in performing that which is best for me both now and eternally! I am alive to the world and very easily taken up with the objects of sense; but O how heavy and dead I am in attending to the duties of my Lord, which are the joy and glory of all the hosts of heaven!

My soul clings to the dust; make me alive, O Lord, according to your Word and to your precept which commands us to be spiritually-minded and to be fervent in spirit, serving the Lord. Make me alive, O my God, according to the Word of your promise, in order that sin may not rule over your servants and that you will achieve in them your perfect will.

Dear Lord, be pleased to perfect that which concerns my soul, and let the love of my heart be to do what you want. Let it be my delight to do your will, O God, and with enthusiasm to observe your commands. O help me to engage myself vigorously and actively in your holy ways, and to perform your blessed will not only because I must, but because it is the desire of my soul, and the joy of my heart to be so engaged.

Let nothing in the world give me so much pleasure and satisfaction as to have my heart approved by you, my God, and to have all my works acceptable in your sight, through Jesus Christ, my only Mediator and Advocate. *Amen.*

19. For God's assistance

O Lord God Almighty, you give power to the weak and increase the strength of those who have no might, without you I can do nothing. I am unable even to will or think anything that is good or to keep myself from anything that is evil, but my help is in the name of the Lord who made heaven and earth. You, O my God, are able to keep me from falling and to make me perfect in every good work, and to work in me that which is well-pleasing in your sight, through Christ Jesus.

You have encouraged me to come boldly to the throne of grace so that I may obtain mercy and find grace to help me in time of need. Lord of all power and grace, I come, trusting in your almighty strength, your infinite goodness and your gracious promises. I come to ask of you whatever is lacking in me and to obtain grace sufficient for me at this time. Let your good Spirit help my infirmities and strengthen me with power in my inner being so that I may be strong in the Lord and in the power of his might, and do all things as I should, through Christ who strengthens me.

I beseech you, who have been gracious towards me in the past and have brought me to where I am, not to cast me off nor to abandon me to myself — for I am as a reed shaken with the wind, a leaf blown to and fro: but to let me continue to experience your help and to find you to be an all-sufficient God, performing all things for me. I will go forth in the strength of the Lord God, and trust in the Lord Jehovah in whom is everlasting strength.

O my Lord, come to my assistance and be my helper! Carry me forward in your holy ways and make all that I think, speak, and do, acceptable in your sight. O may I strive to stir up the grace of God that is in me and let me always find such supplies of grace that I may see my desires accomplished and my efforts fruitful, through Jesus Christ our Strength and Redeemer. *Amen.*

20. For a sense of God's presence

O Lord, the infinite, incomprehensible God, you are the high and holy One who inhabit eternity and dwell in unapproachable light. From your glorious throne in heaven you look down upon all who dwell on earth to give to every one his due reward according to his ways and the fruits of his doings. Though no mortal eye can see you and no finite understanding understand you, yet you are here and everywhere present. Now and always you see us and understand our thoughts from afar and are thoroughly acquainted with all our ways. Yes, you are so universally observant as to have a particular concern for every person and action in the whole world. Great God, you fill heaven and earth with your presence. O fill my heart with your grace and with constant remembrance of your presence with me that I may set the Lord always before me and always remember you in all my ways.

O that I should ever forget the God who made me, the God who gives life to everything that lives, energises everything that moves, and upholds everything that has life throughout the world! O that I should have been, as it were, without you in the world and forgetful of you in whom I live and move and have my being, and who has watched over me for good all the days of my life! Holy God, because I have disregarded you, you might make me aware of your presence in just judgements sent to me. But, O Lord, in mercy pardon all such sinful neglect and inattentiveness.

As I am always exposed to your all-seeing eye, make me to walk as in your immediate presence. Let the remembrance of your presence direct and guide me in secret and in public view, at all times and in all places, and in all my actions. Let me conduct myself as always under the watchful eyes of the great God of heaven and earth and fear you above all other powers, love you above all other gods, serve you before all other lords and trust in you more than in any other refuge. Yes, let me rejoice in the shadow of your wings and here find peace in the knowledge that you are at my right hand and always with me. O let not the remembrance of my Lord be grievous to me but let my meditations of God be sweet as well as frequent that in delighting myself in the Lord, you may give me the desires of my heart. So guide me with your eye that I may not depart from your laws but be ever accepted in your sight through Jesus Christ. *Amen*.

21. For true devotion

O most high and holy Lord God, you will be hallowed in those who come near to you. You are greatly to be feared and to be held in reverence by all who are round you. Be pleased to make me holy with your grace and help me so to draw near to you in prayer that you may draw near to me in communicating your love and mercy.

I desire, O my God, to meet you in your ways and (in compliance with your gracious appointment) I fall down and worship here at your footstool in the name and through the mediation of your dear Son. I am indeed most unworthy to come into your holy presence and utterly unable (by myself) to perform any service worthy to be presented to your heavenly Majesty!

O let your great mercy overlook my unworthiness and keep me from everything that would make my prayers an abomination to the Lord. As you have made me aware of my duty and of my own insufficiency to do it as I ought, O let your good Spirit help my weaknesses. Let your almighty power keep me from sinful dulness and distractions, that I may worship you in spirit and in truth and offer you a sacrifice that shall be well-pleasing in your sight, through Jesus Christ our Lord. *Amen*.

22. For enjoyment of God's gracious presence

O infinite Majesty of heaven and earth who is never absent from anywhere but fills all things with his presence! No place is so desolate as to be without you, no men so bad, as not to live and move and have their being in you. Yes, the very devils are not out of your reach but are aware of your presence though it is to their cost. Even in hell you are there!

But to your people who bear your image, know your voice and prize your love, you are pleased to reveal yourself in a special manner and to visit them as the children of your family. You have promised that you will not leave them comfortless but will come to them and dwell in them and be their God and make them your people. Thus you show yourself to them as you do not show yourself to the world. But the ungodly are far from you, and live without you in the world. Yes, Lord, our sins do make a wall of separation between you and us and for them you might in justice forsake us and cast us off in your displeasure. How justly might you hide your face especially from me and abandon me to my wretched self! But though I deserve such wrath against me, let my wretchedness move you to be compassionate towards me. Where you cannot take pleasure in me, O Father of mercies, have pity on me. Cast me not away from your presence and do not abhor me: I ask this on the basis of that mercy which has moved you to do so much for me already.

O come to me and make your abode with me and rejoice over me to bless me. My soul is as a desolate wilderness, yes, even the very image of hell, without you, my God. O Emmanuel, God with us, for your mercy's sake and for the sake of your promise see me far away and bring me near through the blood of your cross. O bring me out of my present state of alienation from you and make me safe under the shadow of your wings and happy in the embrace of your love.

If you reject me, O my God, what in the whole world can then avail or make any recompense for the loss of your favour? In your favour is life; without it I am dead while I live and shall be forever condemned when I die. But if you are with me and cause the light of your face to shine upon me, I shall overflow with unspeakable joy. Even in the absence of all other friends and comforts I shall not need nor desire them. If only I can go to God, my exceeding joy, and be taken up with my blessed Lord, I shall lack nothing; I can want nothing for in your presence is fulness of joy for evermore.

O blessed are they whom you choose and cause to draw near to you and who are so highly favoured by you, for your presence can make the poorest cottage better than the stateliest palace and fill the hearts of your servants with divine delights to which the greatest men of the world are strangers. O what manner of love is this, that the great God of heaven should condescend to visit and reside with poor mortals on earth! But Lord, how unworthy am I that you should come under my roof! O blessed Jesus! Be pleased to see me as nothing without you, and to note my restless longings for you, and be pleased to come to me, dear Lord, not because I deserve it but because I need you, not for my merits but for yours.

My Lord and my God, whom have I in heaven but you? There is none upon earth that I desire apart from you. O be not as a stranger to the soul in which you have placed an inclination to serve you, but bless and honour me with that divine fellowship of which you have made me capable and which my soul longs for. O give me the satisfaction to find what you have given me the heart to seek. Yes, give me grace, O my Lord, to go on seeking till I find you whom my soul desires above all to love. Let me endure anything rather than your absence and displeasure and desire nothing so much as your presence and favour.

Be not far from me, O my God, but let me experience your gracious presence with me and see your goodness before me. Lord Jesus, you have promised to be with your people even to the end of the world. O come, be with my spirit, and dwell in my heart by faith. Be with me, O my Saviour, everywhere and at all times, in health and in sickness, in prosperity and in trouble, in all states, and in all events and circumstances of my life. Let your presence make holy and sweet to me whatever befalls me. Never leave me nor forsake me in my present pilgrimage; but, abide with me till you have brought me safely through all trials and dangers to your heavenly kingdom, that I may dwell there in your sight and enjoy your love and inherit your glory forever. *Amen*.

23. For heavenly comfort

O most blessed Lord, the God of all consolation, you comfort those who are cast down; you give peace and joy which the world can neither equal nor take away. I confess myself unworthy of one gracious look from you or of one glimpse from the light of your face upon my soul. I deserve to be cast down because of my sins and to groan under their oppressive burden all my days, until at last I go down in sorrow to my grave. But because you know, Lord, that our spirits fail when your face is turned from us, and that we cannot continue with faithfulness and liveliness in your way unless we have that joy in the Lord which is our strength, I beseech you, O Lord of love, to give me a peaceful conscience and say to my soul that you are my salvation. Let your heavenly consolations fortify me against the desire for all sinful pleasures, and make me faithful from the heart to your covenant. O give me some tokens of your love, some disclosures of the light of your face, some experience of that joy which rejoices always.

My soul thirsts for you, my God, to experience your power and glory, even as I have seen you in the sanctuary. How long will you forget me, O Lord? How long will you hide your face from me? How long shall I reason within my soul whilst daily there is sorrow in my heart? O cause your face to look upon me and let my heart rejoice in you because I have trusted in your holy name. Let my mouth be filled with your praise and with your honour all day long. Let my soul be satisfied as with the richest of foods when I praise you with joyful lips.

Whatever is my share of the common favours which you

give freely to all humanity, O remember me, also, O Lord, with the special favour which you confer on your elect people and visit me with your salvation. Let me see the good of your chosen people and rejoice in their gladness and inheritance. O that, renouncing all confidence in myself, I may rejoice in Christ Jesus and count your love better than wine and prefer it more than any earthly joy. Since the result of righteousness is peace, and the effect of it is quietness and assurance for ever, O make me a true and faithful subject of that spiritual kingdom in which dwell righteousness, peace, and joy in the Holy Spirit. Let me taste and see that you are gracious. Let me have such obvious tokens of a divine influence upon my soul, and such an evident witness of your Spirit within me (which will give me heartfelt assurance of your love and favour to me in Christ Jesus), that my soul will bless you, O Lord, and all that is within me will praise your holy name. Let the comfort with which you comfort me also be the means of comforting others and of encouraging them to devote themselves to your service, so that you, the blessed giver of all joy and comfort, may in all things be glorified, through Jesus Christ. *Amen*.

24. For heavenly-mindedness

O blessed God, you alone can satisfy and make our souls happy. In you only, the desires of our hearts find that rest and calm which the whole world can never give. But, alas, this world and the things of it have had too much sway over my thoughts and my heart, so that my affections have diminished and my feelings have grown cold towards you, my God, and to those things which are most worthy of my love. I have pursued eagerly the vanities and trifling concerns of this present time, but O how slack and lacking in desire I have been in the things which eternally concern me! I have been taken up with this world as if it would never end, and forgetful of the next as if it should never begin!

I have forsaken the spring of living water and have dug my own cisterns which can hold no water. I have disturbed myself in vain, seeking rest; and found none, because I have sought it where such a precious treasure cannot be found. How justly O Lord, might you leave me to reap the result of my own wretched choice, to eat its fruit and be filled with its own pleasures! How justly might you reward me solely in this life, which I have so foolishly preferred, and shut me out of that heavenly kingdom which I have so madly despised.

But, O Father of mercies, forgive my defective love for you and my excessive love of earthly things. Diminish, I pray, my desires for these inferior things that, instead of doting upon the world, I may covet earnestly the best gifts, and seek first the kingdom of God and its righteousness, esteeming godliness the greatest gain and all else but as loss and dung, for the love of Christ and the glories of heaven. O show me so much of those great and glorious things of the world to come that my affections for the things of this present world may be deadened. Crucify the world to me and me to the world, that being thus disengaged and loosened from it, I may be filled with more love and enthusiasm for the things above where Christ sits at the right hand of God.

O let me not debase my heavenly soul, by grovelling in the earth as if I had nothing to do but to serve this earthly, sinful body. Enable me to despise the most tempting enjoyments of this world and to find my happiness in the service of the Lord and in the hope of his glory. May my heart be with my treasure in the heavens and let me be always looking for that blessed hope and the glorious appearance of the great God and our Saviour, Jesus Christ. May I not covet great things in the world nor desire to continue long in it, but seek to get safely out of it, desiring to be transformed and to be forever with the Lord. Even so, come Lord Jesus. *Amen and Amen.*

25. *For greater concern for eternal realities*

O Lord God, to whom I am indebted for all that I am or
have, you have given me life and many opportunities and
advantages for working out my salvation. O what else have
I to do upon earth except to prepare myself for heaven? Here
I am placed between an eternity of happiness and an
everlasting life of misery. O what should be my care and
constant endeavour but to flee from the wrath to come and
to lay hold on eternal life, to provide well for my everlasting
condition, and lay a sure foundation for my immortal soul
in this present life, the only time for preparation.

But O how negligent and careless I have been in that which
should concern me most, doing everything rather than this
great work for which you created me. As a result, you may
justly call upon me at any time, O Lord, to give my last
account at an hour and on a day when I did not expect it.
But for the sake of your mercy in Christ Jesus which has
caused you to spare me for so long, go on, I beg you, O
my God, to be merciful to me in forgiving me all my past
laziness and negligence. Stimulate me to be more greatly
concerned and more persevering, that I may regain the time
I have lost and make the best use of every present experience
for my soul's eternal advantage.

O preserve me from all the distracting cares and the sinful
pleasures of this life. Let me look less upon the temporal
things that are seen and turn my eyes towards the invisible
and eternal things of which I am aware. O give me greater
concern for my everlasting state and greater commitment
to the work which, above all else, needs to be done. O let
me dread the doom which awaits the lazy and inactive
servant and not be indifferent to the most important business
of serving the Lord.

O Lord, show me the truth and reality of things to come,
and give me such an understanding of what is my real and
supreme good that my desires for it may be intensified in
proportion to its worth and excellency. Make me so

dissatisfied without it that I may count nothing too much to do, nothing too hard to endure so that I may at last attain the blessed enjoyment of it.

O let the meditation of hell be a deterrent to preserve me from all the ways leading to that dreadful end. May I so look to the joy set before me that I may cheerfully and vigorously exert myself to possess it. O my God, give me the spirit of wisdom from above to discern the immense difference between the brevity of this present time and the infinite duration of immortality, between the pleasures of sin which last for a short time and those heavenly pleasures which are forever. Seeing that this present world must be dissolved, make me a holy and godly person, looking for and hastening the coming of the day of God.

Lift me out of inactivity and procrastination, O Lord, that I may not prolong the time for doing what I am convinced needs to be done to save me from the second death and to bring me to eternal life. O, why am I troubled and careful about many ordinary things when I neglect the one necessary thing? Help me, my God, to use the reason and understanding which you have given to me and to consider calmly what will promote my true happiness. Let me be resolute and faithful to choose to follow it, whatever present difficulties may obstruct my way.

Help me, O Lord, to remember and consider all the powerful inducements which may stimulate me to greater care for my eternal state, that I may spend my time here wisely, preparing for the life to come. Grant, O Lord, that I may work diligently to make my calling and election certain, that I may strive to enter in at the narrow gate and labour for the food that endures to eternal life.

Teach me, O my God, by patiently continuing in your will to seek for glory, honour, and immortality, that I may not lose the rest promised to your people. May I so do your work here that after death I may rest from my labours in your kingdom, not for the merit of my works but for your mercy's sake in Christ Jesus. *Amen.*

26. For a faithful profession of Christianity

O my Lord and my God, you have given me knowledge of
eternal truth, and, by the light of the Gospel shining upon
me, have made the way of salvation plain to me: be pleased
to give me courage to confess you before men and to profess
the faith of Jesus Christ even in the face of an evil and
adulterous generation. O let me not waver or be persuaded
by every new doctrine cunningly created by man to deceive
God's children.

My God and guide, let not the error of the wicked lead
me astray or make me to fall from my commitment; but,
may I ever continue to profess my faith without wavering
and persevere confidently and faithfully to the end. O let
me experience such knowledge and love of your truth that
it may make me faithful always in professing it. Let me not
reject the simplicity that is in Christ or the Faith in which
I have found so much comfort and advantage.

Grant that I may increasingly feel the powerful effects
of it upon my heart, that I may be rooted and grounded
in the Faith and take much pleasure in the way into which
your grace has brought me. Let me never turn from it or
prove myself false to it; but, despite all temptations sent to
seduce or frighten me, may I openly profess it and faithfully
persist in it to my life's end. *Amen*.

27. For enthusiasm as a Christian

O Lord, the holy, jealous God! You have declared that the
lukewarm are loathsome to you, that those who do the
Lord's work deceitfully are cursed, and that a dreadful fate
awaits the slothful servant, who was condemned, not for
committing terrible crimes, but for neglecting to make use
of his talents. You sent us into this world to prepare for
the next and we are a people devoted to the Lord, having
vowed and promised (at our baptism/confirmation) to serve

our God with all the powers and faculties that we possess. This is the one ultimate purpose for which we were made and to which we are strictly bound and which we must follow with our whole hearts if we are to escape the damnation of hell and enter into the joy of our Lord.

But I am ashamed, O my God, that I have loitered so long in your vineyard and trifled so much with your work, that I have occupied myself with vanities and disregarded my greatest business. Well may I now tremble for fear of your judgements when I, as one of the redeemed, have shown such little zeal for good works.

O merciful Lord, forgive all my sinful omissions and all my careless performances of the duties of your service. Awaken within me a greater zeal to promote diligently your glory and to work out my salvation. Let me not strive earnestly only for the faith and doctrine of the Gospel but also for practice of all its duties, that by my way of life I may win others and by my good example I may compel them to glorify my heavenly Father.

To glorify your name and save our souls is our greatest concern in the world. Nothing deserves so much of our care, zeal and diligence as to obtain deliverance from your wrath and to secure possession of your heavenly kingdom. Yet how little we are concerned to be active and to give ourselves wholly to this work when upon it depends an eternity to come; we forget that all that concerns us eternally is fixed in this short life which is so quickly gone and will never return! O my God, imprint these considerations so deeply upon my heart, that I may no more trifle with the weighty things of eternity, nor show a cold indifference to that which is of such absolute necessity. Make me so to act as to be blessed rather than condemned forever. Make me zealous for my God as I have been for the world, as active in the pursuit of eternal things as I have been in the things of this present world. Let me give up myself wholly to you and show the sincerity of my profession by revealing that zeal and fervency which are the very life and soul of Christianity.

O God, the great rewarder of those who diligently seek you; help me to engage seriously in your service and unweariedly to go through with it, not lacking in zeal but fervent in spirit, serving the Lord. Enable me to exert myself to godly living, to be always watchful in prayer, to keep my heart diligent, to have only useful conversations and to run the race set before me with all cheerfulness. O let me do your work with a lively and enthusiastic spirit, full of good works and fruits to your honour, always labouring here to win your favour and your glory hereafter.

O Lord, make me more zealous for your honour than for my own. O let me hate perfectly and oppose strenuously whatever is injurious and reproachful to you, and let me do it with such prudence and kindness towards people, that I may not dishonour my defence of your glory. Let not my zeal consume but inflame my love, nor let it undo all the good that I am able to do for my generation; that I may serve the interests of my Lord and promote the salvation of souls. O make me valiant for your truth and discreet in my conduct, that I may neither betray your holy name by my fear nor become a reproach to it by my folly.

O let me use my zeal and enthusiasm not for earthly but for heavenly things; not for my own desires and honour but for your blessed will and pleasure: not in frivolous contentions about the unessentials and secondary matters of Christianity, but in pursuing the very heart and substance of it; being concerned about the basic and unquestionable duties necessary for the salvation of the soul. Grant me your grace, O Lord, to live now so zealously to the glory of your name that I may come to be blessed forever in the glories of your kingdom, not for the sake of my services but of your mercies, whose gift is eternal life through Jesus Christ our Lord. *Amen.*

28. For grace to serve the Lord with gladness

O my God; you take pleasure in the prosperity of your servants, who in turn have the greatest reason to be pleased in obeying your commands. It is good for me to draw near to God in whose presence is fulness of joy. Well may the hearts of those who seek the Lord rejoice! For you constrain us, not for any advantage to yourself but only for our greatest good that it may go well with us both here and forever. O my Lord, I am very troubled that I should have been so lazy and careless, so weak and so soon weary of your blessed work (to the dishonour of your name and the ill repute of your service) as if I had a hard master and a hateful work. O why do I make into a great burden that which ought to be the solace of my life and the joy of my heart!

Forgive me, I beg of you, good Lord, all this which I confess before you; and heal that tendency of my mind which makes your service a weariness to me. So renew my spirit, and draw my heart to your blessed self that I may serve you from ready desire and not from necessity, not forcing myself but delighting in your work. O rid my mind of that tormenting dread which makes me uneasy in the service of my Lord. Give me a heavenly heart and such a love for your law as will sweeten all my obedience that I may not consider it grievous or tedious but my soul's satisfaction and great joy. O let me not serve you, my God, with the spirit of bondage as a slave but with the cheerfulness and gladness of an innocent child, trusting and delighting in your presence and so pleased with your work that my services may also be acceptable in your sight, through Jesus Christ. *Amen*.

29. For wisdom to have good relationships

O Lord my God, I desire to humble myself in your sight for all the folly and dishonour of my conduct. I have frequently failed in it and so shamefully treated my fellow creatures. My example has too often tended to harden rather than to convert sinners. I have been as a stone that causes them to stumble and as a rock that makes them fall. Not only am I prone to be tempted and overcome with evil myself, but also I become a temptation and a snare to others so as to entice them to sin or to encourage them in it. Though you have shown me what is good, given me knowledge of better things and laid the greatest obligation upon me to be faithful to your covenant, yet how ready I have been to lose my desire for the things of God! How eager to be carried into folly with the stream of evil company, basely to comply and consent with sinners to do evil!

O my God, give me repentance and pardon for all my sins and for all the guilt which I have accrued in being an accessory to the sins of others. So fortify me with your grace that I may not be terrified or tempted away from the path of duty, that I may never be ashamed to confess Christ before men, but boldly to acknowledge your truth even before an evil and faithless generation. O teach me to deal wisely with those who are outside, and in all kindness towards those who are within, and without offence and prudently with all. Make me wise in the choice and in the enjoyment of my company, in order that they may not be to me, nor I to them, a means of falling into sin. May we be mutually helpful to each other and examples of all that is good and imitable and praiseworthy.

O gracious Lord, make me so faithful to you and to my own conscience that my way of life in the world may never destroy the religious frame of my soul. Let me not be surprised by any bold criticism of your ways nor be turned away from you through the opposition of men. Make me to have little regard for the criticism of mortal and finite men. O turn my fear of men's faces into love for their souls! Let me esteem them as my fellow servants in your work and fellow travellers on our long journey home. Where I cannot promote their duty and happiness grant, O Lord, that they may not hinder mine, and that when I am not edified, I may not be corrupted by them.

O my God, may your presence have ever greater influence over me than the presence of men. Let me count it a small thing to be judged by them, and instead of being persuaded by their ways or whims, let me value my own conscience more than their opinion, and do my duty heartily as unto the Lord in the sight of God. Let it not be my aim to ingratiate myself with men but to please the great Judge of all. Yet keep your servant from giving scandal and offence to any, that I may not, by pride and passion, by vanity and indiscretion, or by bad temper and uncharitableness dishonour my profession or cause the way of truth to be unjustly criticised.

Help me, O my God and guide, to walk uprightly, and to speak and act with due consideration at all times and places, and of all persons and in all circumstances. Enable me to behave myself wisely and guide my affairs with discretion, so that I may live amongst my fellow human beings in such a way as to preserve my integrity in your sight, to have my citizenship in heaven, and still enjoy friendship with you and with your dear Son, my only Lord and Saviour. *Amen*.

30. For grace to speak aright

O Lord our gracious God, you have given us reason and speech to communicate and converse freely with one another; we have much reason to praise you because we are so mysteriously and wonderfully made! Our tongues, which are our glory, function according to your design when we use them to set forth your glory. But alas! I have good reason to humble myself for all the abuses of my tongue, for the many ways in which I have perverted the happy privilege of speaking (either holding my peace when I should have spoken to your honour and the good of my neighbour, or else pouring out words to dishonour your name, to wrong my own soul, and to offend and injure others!). Forgive me, O merciful God, I beseech you, all my sinful silence, my vain and idle words, and my evil, corrupt communications. Help me so to speak that I may reveal your grace in my heart and extend the same to my hearers. Watch over my mouth, O Lord, and guard my speech that nothing may proceed from my mouth except what will be good for edifying others.

Help me to keep my mouth with a bridle when I am provoked to speak inadvisedly, and let no unholy or filthy speech proceed from my mouth nor any thing be said by me which is unbecoming for a Christian.

O Lord, open my lips that my mouth may declare your praise. Make me bold to speak for you and for the promotion of truth and the glory of your name; but, make me slow to speak any evil by which I may defile myself or hurt my neighbour. Give me, O Lord, a mind which considers carefully what is fit to be said. Make me wise and serious, sober and modest, pious and charitable in what I speak that it may be without offence, but not without profit, to those who hear it. O fill my heart with such grace that out of a good treasure I may always produce something to benefit others and to advance your glory. Put such thoughts into my mind and such words into my mouth that my tongue may be as the pen of an eager writer, to utter things beneficial and acceptable for the good of my friends. Let me never turn my liberty of speech into vain or evil speaking; but let me employ it for wise and noble ends for which it was given – speaking of and for your truth even before the greatest without being ashamed.

O Lord, restrain the blasphemous and brutish generation which speaks against heaven and from whose mouths, like open sepulchres, come forth impieties and impurities to dishonour him who made them, to grieve the souls of your servants, and to spread the corruption of their ungodliness. O make them ashamed for what they have done, and fill their hearts with dread to stop them from doing further harm. Confound the generation which, like vipers that hiss and spit their venom, speak against your holy laws, and give them, I pray, different thoughts and words that they may use their gifts to better purpose. O let those lying lips which speak grievous things proudly and contemptuously against the righteous be put to silence. And let those who fear you, honour your name and speak often to one another, so as to build each other up in the faith for the eternal salvation of their souls, through your gracious goodness to them in Jesus Christ. *Amen*.

31. For perseverance to endure to the end

Eternal God, with whom is everlasting strength, you are able to keep us from falling and to continue the good work begun in us till the day of Christ's return. But Lord, you know how weak and frail I am, how wavering and prone to backsliding, how ready to decline and fall despite all the great things which you have done for my soul. O Lord of love, have pity on my infirmities and strengthen me in my weaknesses. Preserve me, O blessed guardian and protector of your people. O preserve me from the danger of rejecting my faith and keep me from forsaking any good beginning to which your grace has brought me. Put your fear in my heart that I may not depart from you. Make me so securely yours that nothing which happens to me in the world may ever come between you and my soul or turn me from that way of life which leads to heaven. O let me not be amongst those who revert to unbelief and turn towards hell, but of those who believe the gospel for the salvation of their souls.

Lord God, you have begun to show your servant your greatness and your mighty power; go on, I pray you, to work in me for the glory of your name and to perfect that which you have begun. You have been my help; leave me not, nor forsake me, O God of my salvation; but uphold me and I shall be safe and I shall observe your statutes continually. Help me, O my God, yes, establish, strengthen and confirm me. Leave me neither will nor power to resist the gracious designs of your love and mercy for the salvation of my soul. In my frailty I still too often fall into sin but, through your mercy, recall me to repentance. Though I fall, let me not be utterly cast down but uphold me with your almighty hand and keep me by your power through faith to salvation. O make me faithful until death that you may give to me the crown of life. Make me so to endure to the end, that I may be saved and receive the glorious fulfilment of all my hopes, even that blessed end of my faith, the eternal salvation of my soul. *Amen, Amen.*

32. For preparation and readiness to die

Lord, what is our life but a puff of wind that appears for a short time and then vanishes. Even at the longest, how short; and at the strongest, how frail! We may think ourselves most secure yet we know not what a day may hold for us nor how soon you may come and ask for our last account. Then we shall quickly be as water spilt on the ground that cannot be gathered up again; then we shall quickly be snatched away from here and be completely forgotten. Our days are speedily spent and we do not know how near is our last day when our bodies shall be laid in the grave and our souls called to appear before the tribunal of God to receive their eternal lot.

Yet I recall that I have lived in this world as if I should never leave it, unmindful of my latter end! I have not redeemed the time! I have been careless about my soul! I have been negligent in my preparation for life after death! You, O my God, may justly bring my last hour suddenly upon me to surprise me in my sins and to cut me off in my iniquities. But O Father of mercies, remember not my sins against me but remember your own long-standing tender mercies and loving-kindnesses. O remember how short my time is and spare me that I may recover my strength before I go from here and be seen no more. Make me wise that I may understand and consider my latter end, and teach me so to count my days that I may apply my heart to true wisdom. Lord, what have I to do in this world but to prepare myself for the world to come? O that I may be mindful of it and be careful to finish my work before I finish my course!

In the days of my health and prosperity, O that I may remember and provide for the time of trouble, of sickness and of death, when the world's enjoyments lose their attraction for me and prove utterly useless to support and comfort me. Let me never follow any course of living in which I would be loath or afraid to die, but let me see my inner corruptions expire and die that they may never rise up in judgement against me. Enable me so to die to sin daily that I may not die for sin eternally. Instruct me, good Lord, and assist me in my preparation for my dying hour that I may not then be fearfully surprised but may meet it with comfort and composure. Arouse within me a serious concern for that great work and help me to perform it acceptably and successfully. O that I may be fitted for heaven before I leave this earth and have peace with God through Jesus Christ before I depart to that state in which I must abide forever!

O my Lord, make me so ready to meet you at your coming that your appearance may be the source of my hopes, my joys, my desires, and my joyful expectations. May I look and long for that blessed time when you will put an everlasting end to all my troubles and temptations and exchange my present state of infirmity and sin for a state of endless happiness and glory. You, who are my life and my strength, help me so to live that at the hour of death I shall rejoice that I had lived. Help me to be always prepared for death that, at my last day, I may have nothing to do but to die and cheerfully to resign my sprit into your gracious hands. O my Father, hear and answer my humble petitions and let me find a merciful admission to your favour and your kingdom for the sake of my only Saviour Jesus Christ. *Amen*.

6

EPILOGUE

(i) Introduction

Both Jenks and Simeon emphasised the absolute need to repent of sin and believe the Gospel: that is, to be converted. They believed that there were two types of people in the world – the converted and the unconverted. Further, they held that there were many routes into the experience of conversion but that there was one Gospel of God the Father concerning the one Lord Jesus Christ, made effective by the power of the Holy Spirit. Therefore, it is entirely appropriate that the last prayer in this book be a prayer that every Christian can pray – not perhaps immediately after the experience of conversion but some time after, when there has been time for reflection. For every Christian truly desires to praise the Lord God.

(ii) A converted sinner praises God

I will praise you, O Lord my God, with all my heart: and I will glorify your name for evermore. So great is your mercy towards me that you have delivered my soul from the lowest hell. My lips, therefore, shall greatly rejoice when I sing to you, and my soul, which you have redeemed, will boast in the Lord.

For I was in darkness, but now am light in the Lord: I was dead and am alive: I was lost and am found. When no eye pitied me and when I had not a heart to pity myself, then you, O merciful and ever-blessed God, looked upon me and bid me live. O sinful wretch that I am! That I should be taken and others left! I stand amazed at your kindness, O God my Saviour! The great things which you have done for my soul are incomparably more in my estimation than if you had made me into a prince and blessed me with all the riches and glory of the world. For how soon do all these things pass away and perish! But the Word of God, by which I am born again, lives and abides for ever.

The grace of God which brings salvation to my soul is in me as a well of water springing up to everlasting life. O God of all grace, who had such thoughts of mercy towards me, even when I was your enemy and did nothing but forget and provoke you, you will not despise the day of small things: you will not count against me what I have done wrong and you will not cast me away because of my failures, for you have placed a new principle within me and brought my soul from the gates of hell with a prospect of your heavenly glory.

O what great and painful troubles you caused to come upon me! Yet you turned again and refreshed me, bringing me comfort through your rich, renewing mercy. I would have perished for ever if you, O Lord, had not brought me from my state of being dead in transgressions and sins to newness of life. It were better that I had not been born if I had not been born again. O blessed change and mighty work, worthy of God! O the riches of grace and the wonders of divine power and love! What shall I offer to the Lord for this the greatest of all blessings – which I am not able worthily to describe! I can never admire and bless you enough, O my God, for your love for my soul, which you have brought to see the joy of your salvation. How have you tolerated all my dulness and perversity! What efforts have you been forced to use to overcome my reluctance and make me willing to be saved! But you would not allow me to destroy myself, for you put checks in the way of my sins until you had overcome my heart by your almighty grace and brought me into a right relationship with your blessed self.

Bless the Lord, O my soul: and all that is within me, bless his holy name. My God and my Saviour! I was helpless and hopeless; yet you helped and comforted me in my adversity. The fear of hell was upon me: and you have raised me above it and made me rejoice in hope of your glory. I thank you, O Father, Lord of heaven and earth, for you have hidden these things from the wise and prudent and have revealed them to babes.

O who am I, unworthy wretch, that I should be made so happily to differ from others and from my former self? O what have I done that I should be thus distinguished with your saving mercy, when so great a part of the world is still in darkness and in the shadow of death! I am unworthy, O Lord: I am utterly unworthy; but you are infinitely good, and abundant in mercy.

O blessed God of my salvation! Accept the offering of myself, and all my services, together with my thanks and praise for your love to me in Christ Jesus. O what abundant cause have you given me to love and serve you! Grant, I pray, that my life may be entirely devoted to you from this time forward and that, as I have received such mercy at your hands, I may be ever active and unweary in declaring your praise. Let me bless you, O Lord, at all times; and let your praise be continually on my lips as long as I live. Accept me, O gracious Father, and keep me as your own; and make me even fitter for your blessed and everlasting acceptance in Jesus Christ, my Saviour. *Amen.*

The Hodder and Stoughton
Christian Classic Series

The Hodder and Stoughton Christian Classics are original translations, adaptations or abridgements of the great classics of devotional spirituality. Chosen for their reference to the needs of today's Christians, for their theological and spiritual perception and for the timelessness of their message, each of the titles in the series will enrich the faith of the reader.

The Confessions of Saint Augustine
Saint Augustine (Trans. E. M. Blaiklock)
St Augustine's classic testimony to the grace of God.

The Cloud of Unknowing
Edited by Halcyon Backhouse
An anonymous fourteenth-century mystic's experience of knowing and serving God.

On Loving God and The Twelve Steps of Humility and Pride
Bernard of Clairvaux (Editor: Halcyon Backhouse)
A profound reflection on man's response to God's love and a highly entertaining portrayal of human frailty.

The Little Flowers of Saint Francis
E. M. Blaiklock and A. C. Keys (Translated and edited by)
An inspiring and unique collection of St Francis' sayings, stories and teaching.

Pilgrim's Progress
John Bunyan
The spiritual pilgrimage of Christian: the full version in modern English.

The Institutes of Christian Religion
John Calvin (Editors: Tony Lane, Hilary Osborne)
The most important single book of the Protestant Reformation (abridged).

The City Without a Church
Henry Drummond
Classical meditations on practical Christian living.

The Greatest Thing in the World
Henry Drummond
1 Corinthians 13 expounded: a devotional classic on the theme of love.

The Life of Christ
F. H. Farrar (Editor Halcyon Backhouse)
"The work upon the subject. Fresh and full." C. H. Spurgeon. First published in 1874.

Christian Perfection
Fénelon (Editor: Halcyon Backhouse)
How does the Christian become more and more Christ-like?

An Introduction to the Devout Life
Saint Francis de Sales (Editor: Peter Toon)
Careful, practical instruction on how to live a truly God-centred life.

The Spiritual Exercises
Saint Ignatius of Loyola (Editor: Robert Backhouse)
A classic guide to the disciplined spiritual life for use at home or on retreat.

The Dark Night of the Soul
Saint John of the Cross
The hard spiritual journey that leads to union with God.